Becoming a Critical Thinker

Becoming a Critical Thinker

Fourth Edition

Vincent Ryan Ruggiero

Houghton Mifflin Company
Boston   New York

Director of College Survival: Barbara A. Heinssen
Assistant Editor: Shani B. Fisher
Editorial Assistant: Jonathan T. Wolf
Senior Production/Design Coordinator: Sarah Ambrose
Manufacturing Manager: Florence Cadran
Marketing Manager: Barbara LeBuhn

Cover illustration: Susan Turnbull

College Survival
A Program of Houghton Mifflin Company
2075 Foxfield Drive, Suite 100
St. Charles, IL 60174

Photos: chapter openers, pp. 1, 35, 65, 89, 107, 131, 175 image Copyright © 2001 PhotoDisc, Inc.; Chapter 6 photos, pp. 137, 143, 145, 157, 160, 163, 165 by Kindra Clineff; p. 154 photo by Jim Whitmer; page 145, *An American Requiem* by James Carroll © 1996 Houghton Mifflin Company; jacket design by Michaela Sullivan, front jacket photograph (large): © AP Wide World Photos, front jacket photograph (small): courtesy of the author.

Printed in the U.S.A.

Library of Congress Control Number: 2001131548

ISBN: 0-618-12206-0

123456789-B-05 04 03 02 01

Acknowledgments

Many people have contributed to the fourth edition of this book. I would like to thank Amy Johnson, project editor, and Sarah Ambrose production/design coordinator. I am especially grateful for the help of Barbara Heinssen, Shani Fisher, and Jonathan Wolf, my editors at Houghton Mifflin. I also wish to thank the professors who have made helpful suggestions for this edition and/or previous editions:

- Nancy L. LaChance, DeVry Institute of Technology, Phoenix (AZ)

- Lynn E. Walker, Katherine Gibbs School, New York City (NY)

- Marilyn Corzine, Southwest Florida College of Business (FL)

- Glennon Graham, Columbia College, Chicago (IL)

- Joe LeVesque, Northwood University (TX)

- Susan F. Corl, Louisiana State University, Eunice (LA)

- Joel R. Brouwer, Montcalm Community College (MI)

- Cynthia H. LaBonne, Fairleigh Dickinson University (NJ)

- Penny Schempp, Western Iowa Tech Community College (IA)

- Anita Rosenfield, DeVry Institute of Technology, Pomona (CA)

- Matt Schulte, Montgomery College (MD)

- Mary Vacca, Briarcliffe College (NY)

- Marcia Anderson, Metropolitan State University (MN)

- Andrew Scoblionko, DeVry Institute of Technology (NJ)

- Fran Gray, Southwest Florida College of Business (FL)

- Ozzie Dean, DeVry Institute of Technology, West Hills (CA)

- Mary O'Shaughnessy, DeVry Institute of Technology, Long Beach (CA)

Contents

6   Applying Critical Thinking   131

To the instructor

Although the basic format of the book remains the same as in previous editions, this edition includes a number of noteworthy changes:

- A new introductory chapter, "Strategies for Effective Learning," has been added.

- The sections on truth and contradictions in Chapter 1 have been revised and expanded.

- Two new sections, "Be constructive in discussions" and "Present your ideas to advantage," have been added to Chapter 2.

- The sections on argument and evidence in Chapter 3 have been revised and expanded.

- An entirely new chapter, "Solving Problems," has been added.

- Two new sections, "Thinking critically about research" and "Thinking critically about movies," have been added to Chapter 6, "Applying Critical Thinking."

About this book

This book includes numerous opportunities to develop your thinking skills and apply them to real-life situations. These opportunities are of two kinds:

Exercises

These assignments are indicated by a *question mark*. They invite you to examine ideas, draw conclusions, and do related tasks, such as writing an explanation of your findings. Where appropriate, an Internet component has been added. Additional exercises are also available at http://www.hmco.com/college.

Activities

These assignments are indicated by a *light bulb*. They give you practice in applying a certain format for thinking, one that's based on a cycle of observation, reflection, and judgment. The skills and approaches you use in both the exercises and the activities will be useful in practicing critical thinking beyond your involvement with this book.

Strategies for Effective Learning

How much benefit you get from this book, your other textbooks, and your overall educational experience will depend on your ability to learn. You may have heard that this ability can't be learned, that either you have it in your genes or you don't.

That view is wrong!

Sure, some people learn more easily than others, and inborn talent has something to do with their success. But there's another important factor that isn't found in people's genes—the strategies or "tricks" that enhance learning.

Anyone can master these strategies. And doing so makes learning easier and more enjoyable. In this section you'll learn eleven simple, yet powerful, strategies.

Plan your days

Think of time as money and you'll be less likely to squander it.

Each morning (or the night before if you prefer) make a list of things to do and classify them according to importance: (1) tasks that *must* be completed today and (2) tasks to complete if time permits. The few minutes you spend doing this are a wise investment—they will help you keep focused and accomplish more.

As you plan, keep in mind the three axioms of efficiency:

ELIMINATE WHAT NEED NOT BE DONE

SIMPLIFY WHAT MUST BE DONE

COMBINE TASKS WHENEVER POSSIBLE

Refer to your list throughout the day to be sure you are still on track. If, as often happens, events of the day require you to revise your plan, try to maintain your priorities.

Tackle unpleasant tasks immediately

When a task is unpleasant, do you tend to procrastinate? Most people do. You know you have to read that chapter, write that paper, study for the test. You have every intention of doing so. But you manage to find some excuse for not doing it just yet. Perhaps later today, you tell yourself, or better yet, *tomorrow*. As a result, it never gets done in a timely manner.

Procrastination not only prevents you from doing your best. It also adds tension to your life. It's hard to feel contented with yourself when you know that an unpleasant task awaits your attention. And the longer you wait, the larger it looms.

There is a simple solution to this situation. Put unpleasant tasks high on your list of priorities. Whenever possible, tackle them immediately. By doing so, you'll become a more dependable person. Equally important, you'll increase your sense of self-satisfaction.

Chip away at big jobs

Some tasks are just too big to accomplish at one time. For example, for term papers or projects you may have to spend considerable time in the library, conduct interviews with knowledgeable people on campus, outline the paper, and so on. You'll need a special strategy for getting such projects done on time.

The best approach is to break the project into a number of parts. That way you can budget a little time to the project every few days. For example, each time you visit the library for another purpose, you might also consult one information source for your term paper. Similarly, after you have completed your research in small increments and created your outline, you can do the writing one small section at a time.

The advantage of this approach is that when due dates arrive and others are moaning, "I don't think I'll finish on time . . . Why, oh why didn't I start earlier?" you'll be calm and confident.

Take charge of your mind

Is your mind entirely under your control? Most people would answer yes, but many fail to realize just how often they operate on automatic pilot. Uninvited ideas drift in and out of their consciousness. Memories glitter and draw them back in time. Imagination creates pleasant little daydreams.

If you have experienced such mental meandering, you know how absorbing it can be. Minutes, even hours, seem to evaporate. Be honest—how many times have you sat in a classroom for almost an entire period, only to realize that only your body was present—that your mind was somewhere else entirely.

The human mind is prone to distraction and mass culture has made the problem worse by shortening our attention spans. Television camera angles change every few seconds during programs and even more during commercials. This adds up to hundreds of forced attention shifts every hour we watch. Add to those the shifts we create ourselves by clicking the remote, and it's understandable that many people have trouble concentrating for even a few minutes.

How can you take charge of your mind? Become more aware of what it is doing from moment to moment. That way you'll know when you've lost concentration. When that happens, turn your attention back to what you were doing.

Will you ever reach a point where you will be able to concentrate automatically, without effort? No, nobody does. That is because concentrating, like steering a car, involves making constant slight adjustments. The process is necessary whether one has been driving for only a few weeks or for fifty years. Experience does make it easier, however.

Listen actively

Research has repeatedly shown that people retain, on average, less than half of what they hear. That's not good enough to succeed in college (or, for that matter, in most careers). The main reason for this retention problem is that the mind is capable of processing words much faster than people can speak. In other words, in the typical listening situation—such as a classroom lecture—the mind has too little to keep it occupied, so it wanders.

The solution is to change your mental state from active to passive. That is, from merely waiting for information to actively processing information. The way to do this is simple—take notes. Don't try to get every word; you probably can't write fast enough for that. In some cases, you won't even be able to get every sentence. Direct your mind to identify the most important words and sentences (another task to keep it occupied) and record just those.

In addition to improving your listening, taking notes will also provide you with a valuable tool for exam preparation.

Refuse to tolerate confusion

If you don't understand something in class, do you raise your hand and ask for clarification? Many students don't. They would rather remain confused and risk getting a low grade than run the risk of being thought stupid.

To begin with, the risk is much smaller than they imagine. In many cases, it is nonexistent. When one person doesn't understand, the chances are good that others don't either.

Haven't you ever approached fellow students after class and asked them to explain, only to realize they were as confused as you? It happens all the time.

When one student dares to ask for clarification, other students are likely to be grateful. And the instructor is likely to regard the one who asks as conscientious. Why not be that student yourself?

Study efficiently

Would you believe that A and B students often spend less time studying than C and D students? It's true. The fact illustrates an important principle of learning—the amount of time spent studying is less important than the *circumstances*.

Here's how to get the most from your studying:

Choose the right **time.** If you are a "morning person," who jumps out of bed eager to meet the day's challenges, try to make that time of day your study time. On the other hand, if you are a "night owl," arrange your schedule accordingly.

Choose a suitable **place.** The best place is the one with the fewest distractions. You'll study more efficiently in a quiet corner of the library than in the campus snack bar. If there's not too much activity in and around the parking lot, consider studying in your car.

Choose favorable **conditions.** Don't confuse favorable with enjoyable. For example, you may enjoy having the TV blaring or having your Walkman playing, but for learning, quiet beats noisy every time. (It should go without saying that even a little alcohol diminishes the effectiveness of studying.)

You may have to experiment a little to find what works best for you. But the payoff—faster, more efficient learning—is well worth the effort.

Capture insights

Insights are relatively rare and they arrive unexpectedly. What's more, they seldom pay us a return visit, so it's important to be ready to capture them when they come.

Keep a pencil and paper handy at all times. (If you prefer, carry a micro-tape recorder.) Whenever an interesting idea occurs to you—whether about a course you're taking, a relationship, or anything important to you—record it immediately.

Don't be shy about recording your ideas when you are in a group of people. In this day of pagers and cell phones, no one will think it odd if you say, "Excuse me, I've just thought of something important I don't want to forget."

Read for understanding

Reading is much more than running your eyes across the page and recognizing words. It involves grasping the *meaning* of what is written, understanding the relationship of each sentence and paragraph to all the others.

To get more from your reading, follow this approach:

1. Take about five minutes and **skim** the chapter or article. Pay particular attention to the first two paragraphs and the last paragraph; also pay attention to the headings.

2. Take another few minutes and **reflect** on what you found by skimming. Ask yourself: Is the author's main purpose to inform or to persuade the reader? What is the central idea of the piece? (This will usually be stated in the first or second paragraph and echoed in the last one.) What are the secondary ideas? (The headings should suggest them.)

3. Next, **read** the chapter or article. Keep a reasonable pace, neither rushing nor dawdling. Don't underline or highlight anything yet.

4. Finally, **review** what you have read. At this point, you should be clear about what is important and what is not. Mark the piece accordingly.

This approach will take you no more time than one laborious reading would. It may, in fact, take less. But it will increase your understanding of what you have read.

Improve your retention

We rather quickly forget most of what we learn. This is especially true of what we learn from lectures and textbooks. Yet there is a way to increase the amount of material we retain. That way is by summarizing.

To summarize is to express a body of information in significantly fewer words. An article may be reduced to several sentences, an entire book to several paragraphs.

The key to writing good summaries is to limit yourself to the sentences that express important ideas and to omit those that expand upon those ideas.

Turn these strategies into habits

The last few pages have acquainted you with eleven strategies for effective learning. This acquaintance is an important first step, but that is all. In order to profit from these strategies, you must convert them from ideas that you merely understand to *habits that you put to use and expand, both in class and in your preparations for class.* Take a moment now and decide how you will accomplish that task.

1

Mastering the Fundamentals

What is thinking?

You are staring into space, imagining you are headed for the airport. You picture yourself ready for a month's cruise in the Caribbean, your pockets stuffed with cash. Would this mental process be thinking?

Now imagine you're discussing politics with friends. "It's always the same with politicians," you say. "They're full of promises until they're elected. Then they develop chronic amnesia. I can't see why people get excited over elections." Would you be thinking in this case?

Thinking, as we will define it in this book, is a purposeful mental activity. You control it, not vice versa. For the most part, thinking is a conscious activity. Yet the unconscious mind can continue working on a problem after conscious activity stops—for example, while you sleep.

Given this definition, your ruminations about a Caribbean cruise are not thinking but daydreaming, merely following the drift of your fantasies. On the other hand, your discussion of politics may or may not involve thinking. We can't be sure. You might not be thinking at all but just repeating something you'd said or heard before.

Thinking is sometimes regarded as two harmonious processes. One process is the production of ideas (creative thinking), accomplished by *widening* your focus and looking at many possibilities. The key to this process is to resist the temptation to settle for a few familiar ideas. The other process is the evaluation of ideas (critical thinking), accomplished by *narrowing* your focus, sorting out the ideas you've generated, and identifying the almost reasonable ones.

Both processes are natural activities for human beings, but we rarely perform them well without training and diligent practice. This book focuses on evaluating ideas (critical thinking) but also includes some approaches for producing them.

Critical thinking is crucial

Chances are you've received little or no instruction in critical thinking. Your teachers are not to blame for this. In many cases they, and their teachers before them, were denied such training.

Much of our education was built on the idea that thinking can't be taught, or that some subjects teach it automatically. Modern research disproves both ideas. Thinking can be taught—not just to "gifted" students but to all students. No course automatically teaches thinking, though any course can teach it when teachers make thinking skills a direct objective. Then students get regular practice in producing and evaluating ideas. Around the world, schools are exploring ways to make critical thinking a priority.

Success in work depends on thinking skills. It isn't

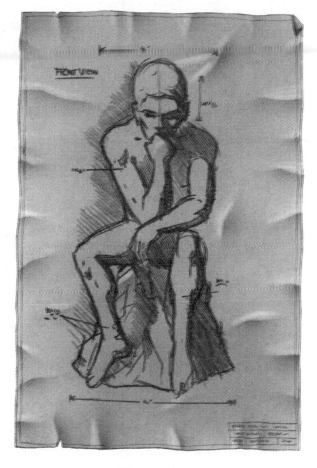

enough for graduates to possess a large body of information in their fields. People who want to succeed must be able to apply what they know to the challenges of their jobs. Employers are looking not for walking encyclopedias but for problem solvers and decision makers.

Mental health also depends in large part on skill in thinking. Some authorities believe neuroses stem from shallow, illogical thinking. According to psychologist Albert Ellis, "Man can live the most self-fulfilling, creative, and emotionally satisfying life by intelligently organizing and disciplining his thinking."

Unfortunately, shallow and illogical thinking is common. For example, the drug or alcohol abuser may say, "I'm not addicted—I can quit any time I want." The skeletal

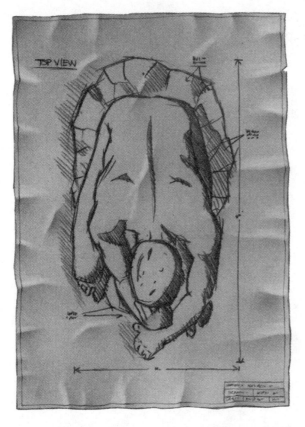

anorexic may tell herself, "I'm too fat." Even highly educated people may reason, "My sexual partners are nice people, so I needn't fear catching a sexually transmitted disease."

Illogical thinking plays a big part in abusive behavior. A parent who makes a child cry by screaming at her may reason that hitting the child will make her stop crying. A Miami woman was charged with dousing her husband with rubbing alcohol and setting him on fire because he had been acting crazy and refusing to work. She reasoned that by setting him on fire she'd get him into the hospital for some help. A father kept his 18-year-old daughter chained in the basement because he was afraid she would become a prostitute.

Occasionally we read in the news about an attempted bank robbery that failed. Surely even slow-witted felons realize that banks have cameras and that getaway cars can usually be identified. Also, every police agency, including the FBI, is involved in bank robbery investigations. Yet the robbers somehow manage to reach the conclusion that they will not be caught.

Even when poor thinking is not tragic, it can be embarrassing. Consider the man who loaned money to his friend, a car dealer. After trying unsuccessfully to collect the money, he reasoned: "I'll take a car from his lot and hold it as collateral. Then he'll have to pay me to get his car back." Proud of his plan, he carried it out . . . and quickly found himself in jail on a charge of grand theft auto. Although the charge was dismissed, his humiliation lingered.

Much unpleasantness and disappointment can be avoided by testing ideas for reasonableness before accepting and acting on them. Such testing isn't just for special occasions. It is appropriate whenever someone makes a claim that is open to question. Many such assertions are made daily in every field of study and work.

Testing ideas is so fundamental to critical thinking that this book includes lots of practice in it. When the ideas are unfamiliar, you will probably be quite willing to examine them critically.

The ideas you will be reluctant to examine critically are likely to be ones you are familiar with, particularly the ideas that are widely accepted in our culture. You will assume that other people tested them. Meanwhile, everyone else may be making the same assumption.

Thus, the more widely held the view, the more it is likely to need critical examination.

Be clear about truth

"There's no such thing as objective truth that's the same for all people regardless of their beliefs."

"Truth is subjective and personal."

"Everyone creates his or her own truth."

Statements like these are quite common today. And they do not mean merely that when we believe something to be true, we act as if it were true. (That would be perfectly reasonable.) Instead, they mean that believing something is so *actually makes it so.*

This idea directly opposes the view of truth that has been generally accepted since ancient times. Here is that traditional view:

> *Truth is objective reality, the actual state of affairs about things. It is un-affected by people's knowledge or ignorance of it, or by their affirmation or denial. No amount of fantasizing or pretending can alter it.*

According to this traditional idea, if a drunk falls into an empty swimming pool, his landing won't be any softer if he believes it is full. If someone accidentally drinks deadly poison believing it is medicine, it won't be any kinder to his body.

These two situations suggest that the traditional view is much more sensible than the popular view that everybody creates his or her own truth. But let's test some more situations to be sure.

When you go to your physician with a health problem, do you want him to *create* the reality of your condition or *discover* it?

Is the Internal Revenue Service likely to accept your subjective, personal truth about your income and deductions, or will they demand the impersonal, objective truth?

If a political officeholder were accused of lying and responded, "No big deal—one person's lie is another person's truth," would you consider that answer reasonable?

Would justice be served if the wording of the standard courtroom oath were changed from, "I swear to tell *the* truth, *the* whole truth, and nothing but *the* truth" to "I swear to tell *my personal* truth . . ."?

Suppose that you got all the test questions correct but received a failing grade anyway and protested to your instructor. Would you be satisfied if she explained, "Your truth was that you deserved to pass. But my truth was the opposite"?

In all these situations, as in the swimming pool and deadly medicine cases, it is ridiculous to speak of *his* truth, *her* truth, *my* truth, *your* truth. All that matters is *the* truth.

Given the popularity of the false notion that truth is personal and subjective, you may have to remind yourself now and then that truth is impersonal and objective. It is something we discover rather than create.

Here is a simple habit that can help you avoid confusion: Use the word *truth* more carefully, reserving it for what is actually so. If an idea is open to question, call it a "belief," "theory," or "contention," not a "truth."

Exercise 1

Apply what you learned in this section to the following situations.

Situation   *In the early seventeenth century, virtually everyone agreed that the sun revolved around the earth. Galileo shocked his contemporaries by arguing that the reverse was true. Would it be reasonable to say that Galileo created a subjective truth, valid for him but not necessarily for others? Explain.*

_____

_____

_____

_____

_____

_____

Situation   *Contemporary admirers of Hitler deny the existence of Nazi concentration camps and a Nazi plan to commit genocide against the Jews. Should that view be considered historically legitimate—that is, true for those who wish to believe it? Why or why not?*

_____

_____

_____

_____

_____

_____

Situation   *Throughout this century, a famous painting entitled* The Man with the Golden Helmet *was believed to be the work of the Dutch master Rembrandt. Some years ago it was proved to have been painted by someone else. Some people would say that the truth about this painting changed. Do you agree? Explain.*

_____

_____

_____

_____

_____

_____

_____

_____

Exercise 2

Examine each of the following cases in light of what you've learned about truth in this section. State your view and explain why you hold it.

Maude smokes a pack of cigarettes a day and drinks alcohol immoderately. Will the belief that she can create her own truth help her change these habits?

_____

_____

_____

_____

_____

Ira is a journalist. Will the belief that he can create his own truth make him more or less likely to value accuracy in his reporting?

_____

_____

_____

_____

Bruce is prejudiced toward minorities and women. Which of the following beliefs would be more helpful in overcoming his prejudice: the belief that truth is subjective and created; or the belief that truth is objective and discovered? Explain your reasoning.

_____

_____

_____

_____

_____

_____

Exercise 3

Imagine you are writing to a friend. Explain what you learned about truth in this section. Use your own words and make your examples different from the ones included here.

_____

_____

_____

_____

_____

_____

_____

_____

_____

_____

_____

_____

_____

_____

_____

_____

_____

_____

Be alert for contradictions

Contradictions are statements that express the opposite of something stated previously. The reason we should remain alert for contradictions is that they signal errors in thinking and provide a starting point for finding those errors.

The principle of contradiction is as follows:

An idea cannot be both true and false at the same time in the same way.

A few examples will serve to demonstrate that this principle is valid.

Statement: My roommate borrowed my sweater without permission.

Comment: If this statement were both true and false at the same time in the same way, it would mean that you simultaneously *gave* your permission and *didn't give* your permission. That is an impossibility. You must either have given your approval or not given it. This example confirms the principle of contradiction.

Statement: During World War II the Nazis killed millions of Jews in concentration camps.

Comment: Either the Nazis did this horrible deed or they didn't. Since there is no way they did it *and* didn't do it, this example also supports the principle of contradiction.

Statement: Capital punishment is a deterrent to crime.

Comment: Let's assume for the sake of discussion that capital punishment was once a deterrent to crime but no longer is. In other words, that this statement was true at one time but is false today. Does this situation challenge the principle of contradiction? No. The principle specifies that a statement cannot be both true and false *at the same time* in the same way.

Statement: Edgar is richer than Clem.

Comment: If Edgar has more money than Clem, but Clem surpasses him in moral character, then the statement would be both true and false but not *in the same way*. It would be true in one sense and false in another. (To be a contradiction, it would have to say Edgar has more money than Clem *and* does not have more money than Clem.) Thus, this example also confirms the principle of contradiction.

A note of caution: The principle of contradiction does not apply to the many *near*-contradictions that occur in everyday discussion.

Let's suppose that Luke says, "Sally got the highest mark on the mid-term exam" and Freda responds, "No, she didn't—Hank did."

That looks like a contradiction, but is it? No. *Sally did vs. Sally didn't* is a contradiction. *Sally did vs. Hank did* is merely a near-contradiction.

The distinction is important because in an actual contradiction one side must be right and the other wrong. In a near-contradiction, *both* sides may be wrong. In the case at hand, the highest mark on the mid-term exam may be neither Sally's nor Hank's but *Bertha's.*

Exercise 4

Classify each of the following dialogues as (a) an actual contradiction or (b) a near-contradiction. Briefly explain each choice.

Mavis: *Big-time college sports are corrupt.*
Cora: *You're absolutely wrong, Mavis.*

_____

_____

_____

_____

_____

_____

Karen: *There are very few real heroes today.*
Hanna: *I think there are more today than there have ever been.*

_____

_____

_____

_____

_____

_____

Brad: *Look at that new Lincoln across the street.*
Clara: *That isn't a Lincoln—it's a Mercury.*

_____

_____

_____

_____

_____

_____

Recognize opinions

O pinions are beliefs or conclusions about reality. Unlike facts, they are open to question
and analysis by critical thinking. Before evaluating opinions, distinguish them from facts.

Sometimes it's easy to separate facts from opinions. "Babe Ruth was a famous baseball player" is
clearly a fact. "Smoking should be banned in public
places" is clearly an opinion. Yet many other statements are more difficult to classify.

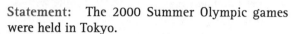

Statement: The 2000 Summer Olympic games
were held in Tokyo.

Comment: This statement has the form of a fact. Yet it is not factual. The 2000
Summer Olympic games were held in Sydney, Australia.

Statement: Camel's hair brushes are made of Siberian squirrel fur.

Comment: The statement appears ridiculous, yet it is factual.

Statement: Stalin's oppression of the Russian people was more brutal than Hitler's
oppression of the German people.

Comment: This statement is an opinion, but it is so well supported by historical
evidence that many would consider it a fact. (Stalin killed more of his own people
than did Hitler. He also took away more freedoms for a longer period than did
Hitler.)

Statement: Eyewitness testimony is generally unreliable.

Comment: This statement is an opinion. To those unfamiliar with the research on
eyewitness testimony it may seem untrue. Yet research confirms it.

Being able to recognize opinions will help you decide when an idea calls for
support and what kind of support is appropriate. This knowledge can help you develop your own ideas and evaluate ideas from others.

Following are some basic guidelines:

1. **If what you state is generally understood to be factual, no support is needed.**

   Example: Both John and Robert Kennedy were assassinated.

   Example: The cost of a college education is significantly higher today than it
   was twenty years ago.

   Comment: Both statements are common knowledge.

2. **If what you state is not common knowledge or can't be easily verified, then briefly note the source of the information.**

   Example: The gray reef shark uses unusual body language to signal that it feels threatened.

   Comment: This fact is not well known, at least among laypeople, so cite the source. (It is Bill Curtsinger, "Close Encounters with the Gray Reef Shark," *National Geographic,* January, 1995, 45–67.)

3. **If the statement is an opinion—a view others might disagree with—then answer any questions others might ask.**

   Example: More Americans are victimized by chronic laziness than by workaholism.

   Comment: However reasonable this statement may seem, some people will undoubtedly disagree. Even those who agree may ask, "Why does the author think this? What cases or examples support this view? Is statistical evidence available? Statements by authorities? What line of reasoning led the author to this conclusion?" Unless these questions are satisfactorily answered, critical readers might not be persuaded.

4. **If it is not clear whether a statement is a fact or an opinion, then treat the statement as an opinion.**

Remember another important point about opinion. As used in critical thinking, opinion refers only to matters of judgment, not to matters of taste or personal preference. The ancient Roman saying *De gustibus non disputandum est* still holds true today. Loosely translated, this saying means "There's no way to argue profitably or think critically about matters of taste."

Do you favor the now-fashionable slender figure or the older ideal of plumpness? Do you find long or short hair more appealing? Do you wear formfitting athletic shorts or the long, baggy kind now standard in basketball? Do you regard the Lincoln Town Car as beautiful or ugly? Do you enjoy sitcoms more than soap operas? All these are matters of personal preference or taste. They can't be supported by facts but only by assertion—"That's my view because that's my view."

As long as you express matters of taste as such, you need not defend them, even if others find your tastes odd. If you express matters of taste as if they were matters of judgment, then you might be in the awkward position of defending what is difficult or impossible to defend. One solution is to say:

"I prefer slenderness to plumpness."
"I prefer long hair."
"I prefer formfitting athletic pants to long, baggy ones."
"I prefer the look of the Lincoln Town Car to that of any other car."
"I enjoy watching sitcoms more than soap operas."

Make statements like these instead of stating that one thing is superior to another.

Exercise 5

Indicate whether each of the following statements is
a) clearly a fact.
b) possibly a fact, but not clear without documentation.
c) an opinion.
d) a personal preference expressed as a personal preference.
e) a personal preference incorrectly expressed as an opinion.
Remember, it is sometimes difficult to separate facts and opinions.
There may be room for disagreement over some answers. Be prepared
to explain your choices.

_____ 1. I find blue-eyed redheads appealing.

_____ 2. The Chevrolet Camaro is the most stylish car on the market.

_____ 3. All religions share the same fundamental truths.

_____ 4. Darwin's theory of evolution continues to be controversial.

_____ 5. Pornography is an insult to women.

_____ 6. Black people are the victims of crime more often than white people.

_____ 7. Prostitution should be legalized.

_____ 8. People who need organ transplants greatly outnumber organ donors.

_____ 9. The publicity given to suicides leads to most "copycat" suicide attempts.

_____10. Comic books are as instructive about life as novels are.

_____11. Most students who drop out of school lack the intelligence to succeed.

_____12. Surgical procedures have been performed on fetuses while they were still in the uterus.

Exercise 6

Now take the statements in Exercise 5 and do as follows:

■ For each that you classified (b), state one or more reliable sources that could be cited to support the statement (assuming that the statement is factual).

■ For each that you classified (c), write questions that might be raised about the statement.

■ If you classified any statement (e), rewrite it as a personal preference rather than as an opinion.

T est opinions

Critical thinking means recognizing and evaluating opinions. Opinion has not always been held in the high regard it enjoys today. Almost 2,000 years ago the Greek philosopher Epictetus wrote: "Here is the beginning of philosophy: a recognition of the conflicts between men, a search for their cause, *a condemnation of mere opinion . . . and the discovery of a standard of judgment.*" Nineteenth-century British author Sir Robert Peel termed public opinion "a compound of folly, weakness, prejudice, wrong feeling, right feeling, obstinacy, and newspaper paragraphs."

American author John Erskine sarcastically termed opinion "that exercise of the human will which helps us to make a decision without information." Poet and philosopher George Santayana observed that "people are usually more firmly convinced that their opinions are precious than that they are true." And one humorist suggested that many opinions that are expressed ought to have gone by slow freight.

Why are these and many other observers so critical of opinion? Because opinions are so easy to form and because shallow, foolish opinions are so difficult to change. Consider how long it took to change the opinions that the earth is flat, that slavery is acceptable, and that cigarette smoking is harmless.

Even experts, who know their subjects in great depth, sometimes form erroneous opinions. It's not surprising that nonexperts err so easily.

Part of the problem is that it's difficult to acknowledge ignorance. When people ask us what we think about something, we are reluctant to say "I don't know." So we express a view and then bond with it, much the same as parents bond with a new baby. Rejecting the idea seems unthinkable. Over the years we may accumulate hundreds or even thousands of opinions that we never test.

Armed with little more than a sketchy news report, an assertion by a celebrity, or a preconception, people state opinions on complex subjects: the cause of child abuse, the reason why dinosaurs became extinct, the benefits of supplemental vitamins, and many more.

Some time ago, a roving reporter took his tape recorder into the street and asked passersby, "How serious is racial tension in New York?" Among those who responded were a porter, two teachers, a truck driver, a film editor, a security guard, and a secretary. Even though these people may have known little about the matter, they still expressed opinions.

There's a great difference between such casual, off-the-top-of-the-head opinions and informed opinions. For example, a physician's opinion about the best way to treat a disease is an informed opinion; so is an accountant's opinion about the legitimacy of a tax deduction, or the Supreme Court's decision on the constitutionality of a law. Critical thinkers in any field develop their opinions with care and test them for reasonableness.

Test some common opinions to see just how reasonable they are. To illustrate the testing process, consider the following statement by a famous psychologist.

The Opinion: "One of the basic things which I was a long time in realizing, and which I am still learning, is that when an activity *feels* as though it is valuable or worth doing, it *is* worth doing." (Carl Rogers)

The Test: Think of a variety of activities that could conceivably feel valuable or worth doing and decide whether they *are* valuable or worth doing.

The Activities:

(a) Sending a sympathy card to a friend whose parent has just died

(b) Lying about your education and work experience on a résumé

(c) Lending money to your brother or sister

(d) Shoplifting

(e) Telling your parents how much you appreciate them

(f) Starting a nasty rumor about your ex-boyfriend or ex-girlfriend

(g) Seeing how fast your car will go

(h) Telling your boss what you think of him or her

The Decision: Feelings sometimes guide us well (a, c, e) but sometimes do not (b, d, f, g, h). Therefore, Rogers's opinion is unsound.

This is not the only test we could conduct. Another would be to ask whether trusting feelings helps prejudiced people become fair minded, wife beaters stop their abuse, or envious people overcome jealousy. We can also ask whether trusting feelings makes people more forgiving, marriages stronger, and neighborhoods safer. Since following feelings *leads* to such problems, it is unlikely to *solve* them.

Opinions can express important truths and serve as building blocks to knowledge. However, opinions can also confuse and mislead, obstructing genuine insights. Critical thinkers understand that having a right to an opinion does not mean that every opinion is right.

Carry out the test specified in each of the following exercises.

Exercise 7

The Opinion: "With the right motivation anyone can achieve excellence in any field of endeavor."

The Test: Think of a variety of activities and a number of different people you know (or know of). Decide whether the opinion applies in each case.

The activities:

_____

_____

_____

_____

The decision:

_____

_____

_____

_____

Exercise 8

The Opinion: A famous movie actress explained her decision to nurse her child until she was two years old: "That's a particular philosophy I have . . . allowing her to make her own decisions. I feel she is a better judge than I am."

The Test: Check what studies in child psychology reveal about a one- or two-year-old child's ability to decide. Visit the library and consult one or two child psychology books. Then decide whether the actress's opinion is reasonable.

The experts say:

_____

_____

_____

_____

Your decision:

_____

_____

_____

_____

Evaluate evidence

It is possible to evaluate opinions even when they are stated alone, without supporting explanations. More commonly, though, people offer information to bolster a case. Such information, called *evidence,* comes in a variety of forms.

In informal writing and discussion, evidence may be nothing more than a simple statement of one or more reasons: "I believe this because. . . ." More often, evidence includes details about past events or incidents and references to observations or written accounts. Formal presentations frequently include experimental and statistical evidence as well.

In evaluating evidence, the focus is not on the opinion itself but on the quality of the support that is offered. Persuasive evidence demonstrates that the stated opinion is more reasonable than other opinions.

Example: That exam wasn't fair because it tested us on material that we were specifically told we weren't responsible for.

Comment: The evidence, if accurate, is persuasive. (Teachers have an obligation to keep their word.)

Example: I'm inclined to dismiss that story about Elizabeth Taylor as false. After it appeared in a supermarket tabloid, no other newspaper or broadcast agency picked it up.

Comment: The evidence, if accurate, is persuasive. Such tabloids have a reputation for misleading and exaggerating their reports. It is therefore reasonable to be cautious in accepting what they say, particularly when other news sources do not confirm the story.

Example: We acted properly in installing surveillance cameras in the employee lounge and restrooms because we have a right to identify troublemakers in the firm.

Comment: The evidence—the claim of a right to identify troublemakers—would be sufficient if no conflicting rights were involved. That is not the case. Employees also have the right to privacy. To be persuasive the evidence must also show that the employer's right outweighs the employees' rights.

Example: Taking money from my employer's petty cash fund isn't really stealing. My employer pays me less money than the person I replaced. He has also given me more responsibilities. And if I didn't take that money, I wouldn't be able to pay my bills.

Comment: Even if all three of the statements offered in support of the opinion are true, they are not persuasive. Stealing is defined as taking something belonging to someone else without that person's permission. The evidence offers an explanation of *why* the person stole (a weak explanation at that). But the act still constitutes stealing.

Even if the evidence presented is unpersuasive, the opinion could still be reasonable. Other evidence that is not presented might make that clear. Suppose a friend says to you, "That car salesman must be dishonest. He's just too smooth and accommodating." That evidence is unpersuasive. It's possible to be smooth, accommodating, and honest. Even so, the salesman may be dishonest. To decide whether he is, ask for more evidence than your friend presented. For example, find out whether the salesman accurately describes a car's features, available options, and safety ratings.

Familiarity can be a serious obstacle to critical thinking. When we agree with an opinion, we may easily approve any evidence offered in support of it. Conversely, when we disagree with an opinion, we may tend to reject even solid evidence. To judge evidence fairly, resist these tendencies. This task is difficult, calling for special care and attention. (For a fuller explanation of evidence, see pages 67–68.)

Exercise 9

In each of the following cases, the first sentence states an opinion, and the second sentence states supporting evidence. Decide whether the evidence shows that the stated opinion is more reasonable than any other. If the evidence is faulty and you have evidence that would support the opinion, state that evidence.

a) *Your Honor, I believe I was justified in hitting my wife. She kept nagging me about getting a job.*

b) *I didn't sign that petition. The person who asked me to sign refused to support my proposal last year.*

c) *I oppose the health care proposal. It restricts people's freedom to choose their own physicians.*

d) *I recommend that we promote Martha rather than Bill. Our company doesn't have enough women in the upper levels of management.*

_____

_____

_____

_____

e) *I oppose government funding for abortions. It requires taxpayers to finance a procedure that many of them believe is a moral outrage.*

_____

_____

_____

_____

f) *Students who are caught cheating should receive a failing grade in the course. Cheating is a serious violation of scholarly integrity.*

_____

_____

_____

_____

g) *Women should not take their husbands' names when they marry. Doing so is a sign of subjugation.*

_____

_____

_____

_____

h) *Drugs should be legalized. Enforcing the nation's drug laws has proved an impossible task.*

_____

_____

_____

_____

Dare to change your mind

Changing your mind means admitting that your prior view was mistaken. This admission is seldom pleasant, and many people go to great lengths to avoid it. But critical thinking demands that honesty be valued more than pleasant feelings, and that opinions be revised whenever the evidence suggests they are mistaken.

Some people have the idea that critical thinkers have no convictions. This idea is mistaken. It would be foolish for critical thinkers to take the time and trouble to find sound answers to important questions and then refuse to embrace those answers with confidence.

If anything, critical thinkers prize convictions more highly than do others. They form opinions carefully and are willing to reconsider those opinions whenever they encounter conflicting evidence. They reconsider even their most cherished opinions in this way.

In contrast, uncritical thinkers form opinions casually. These thinkers treat every opinion as if it were a conviction and every conviction as if it were unquestionable. They applaud the wisdom of views that support their own. When uncritical thinkers encounter an opposing view, they become defensive and assert their opinions more forcefully. Hoping to avoid embarrassment, they actually increase it!

To avoid this mistake, keep the following facts in mind:

Your opinions and convictions do not own you; you own them. And any time you find an opinion to be lacking in quality, you have a right to discard it. When you change your mind and admit your mistake, you demonstrate courage and integrity.

If you form opinions carefully, you may often find that re-evaluation confirms them. That is to be expected. But remember that everyone is wrong on occasion. So if your re-evaluation always confirms your original opinions, consider the possibility that you are unconsciously twisting the evidence in your own favor.

A sample issue

Consider an actual issue and see how a critical thinking approach works:

Jennifer begins to wonder whether her view of astrology is reasonable. Here is her view:

I think astrology is a good guide to everyday living. Newspapers, magazines, radio, and television treat it seriously. Many well-known, educated people use it to make decisions.

Seeking more evidence, Jennifer visits the library and discusses the project with the librarian. With his help she finds a number of books and articles, some supporting astrology and others rejecting it. She also checks the Internet, and interviews a professor of psychology and a professor of comparative religion. Finally, she consults the Yellow Pages and calls a local astrologer.

After evaluating her reading and discussion, Jennifer changes her initial view. Her revised view and supporting evidence follow:

Many well-known, educated people believe in astrology. Even so, I think it's an ineffective guide to everyday living. One reason is that astrology is based on superstitions of a primitive time. For example: "Because Mars is red, it is associated with blood and aggression."

Another reason is astrology's argument that planets influence us at the moment of birth. Science has shown beyond question that the moment of conception is a more important time.

A third reason is that astrologers offer no answer to this question: If the planets Uranus, Neptune, and Pluto were discovered after 1780, weren't all horoscopes before that time necessarily wrong?

By having the courage to change her mind when the evidence called for it, Jennifer gained assurance that her opinion can withstand discussion and debate.

Exercise 10

State your present opinion on each of the following issues and the evidence for that opinion. Consider alternative views—perhaps by going to the library, conducting interviews, or researching on the Internet. Decide whether another opinion is more reasonable than yours and explain your answer below. Attach a separate sheet of paper identifying your sources—for example, publications, individuals you interviewed, and web site addresses.

a) Should athletes be required to meet the same entrance standards as other students?

_____

_____

_____

_____

_____

_____

b) *Should the federal government pass laws to prohibit pornography on the Internet?*

_____

_____

_____

_____

_____

_____

c) *Should schools or companies have policies limiting use of the Internet to school- or work-related activities?*

_____

_____

_____

_____

_____

_____

_____

A comprehensive thinking strategy

All the aspects of critical thinking discussed in this chapter are important. Also important is an overall strategy for dealing with everyday situations. The strategy presented in this section can help you develop valuable insights and skills. It includes three steps:

1. Observe

2. Record your observations

3. Address relevant questions

Step 1: Observe

Good ideas spring more readily from a mind filled with knowledge than from an empty mind. The better you take note of the world around you, the better you can think. Pic-

ture your mind as a tree with branches reaching upward and outward. Branches grow only if the tree's roots extend deep and wide. Those branches are ideas; the roots are knowledge.

Knowledge comes through the senses, particularly sight and hearing. To observe means to detect the issues being discussed, the opinions expressed about those issues, the evidence offered in support of those opinions, and the various disputes that have arisen.

One arena for observation is your everyday contacts with other people at home, in school, at work, and in the community. Active listening there can bring you valuable knowledge and improve your personal relationships.

Another arena for observation is printed material—newspapers, magazines, and books. Spend a little time each day keeping up with local, national, and world events. At the very least, consult the editorial pages of a good newspaper. Read the editorials, letters, and business columns. Don't read passively, waiting for understanding to jump out at you, but actively, looking for meaning.

In reading longer works, such as magazine articles and books, extend your concentration. Don't be discouraged if you encounter distractions. Everyone does. Concentrating is like driving a car down a curvy highway. We turn right, then left, making small corrections to keep the car on the road. Like a car, the human mind needs steering to stay on course. When distractions occur, refocus your attention. With practice, your concentration will improve.

Nonprint media are a third arena for observation. These include movies, television, radio, and the Internet. Use of the Internet has increased dramatically in recent years, and from every indication, this trend will continue.

Several centuries ago, Francis Bacon argued that the purpose of reading is neither to agree nor to disagree with what is said but to weigh and consider it. That is good advice when using nonprint media as well.

Step 2: Record your observations

Critical thinking entails reflecting on the meaning and significance of observations and the reasonableness of ideas. It would be nice if we could call a time-out whenever we wanted to reflect on something that happened or was said. Then life would come to a standstill until we were ready for it to resume.

Alas, we don't have that option. Time moves at its own pace. Hours may pass before we can spare time for reflection. By then we may have forgotten what happened or what about it we found interesting. That is why for most people the habit of reflection remains a good intention and not an accomplishment. A solution to this dilemma is to record interesting observations as they occur so that you can reflect on them later.

The best way to do this is to keep a journal. This chapter will demonstrate how to do so and invite you to begin your journal. You'll find space at the end of each chapter for this kind of critical thinking practice and specific directions for doing it.

After you complete this book, you may wish to continue keeping a journal. Select a bound notebook no smaller than 6 × 9 inches, or use the computer journal form shown at **http://www.hmco.com/college**. Use the left pages for recording observations and the right pages for reflections on those observations. Leave extra space for reflections so you can expand them.

Following are kinds of observations to include and the kinds of reflection to aim for:

Observation: Interesting issues you would like to address when you have more time.

Reflection: Identify the various views people take on the issues and the evidence they offer in support. Find additional evidence, if possible, and decide which view of the issue is most reasonable.

Observation: Statements that appear to be unusually insightful. (You may have read the statements in a book, heard them from instructors or fellow students, or encountered them on television or the Internet.)

Reflection: Think of appropriate ways to test the statements to determine whether they are in fact insightful. Carry out the tests. (Be prepared to modify or even reverse your first impression.)

Observation: Statements that you suspect are shallow or mistaken because they are not supported by your experience.

Reflection: Think of appropriate ways to test the statements to determine whether they are in fact shallow or mistaken. Carry out the tests. (Be prepared to modify or even reverse your first impression.) If you wish, frame a response to any statement that proves to be shallow or mistaken.

Observation: Anything you experience or hear about that you wish to understand more fully—for example, an incident, a process, or a procedure.

Reflection: Decide how best to learn more about the matter. Apply yourself to that end.

Note that in all these situations your knowledge is incomplete or unsatisfactory. Statements or situations "appear" or "seem" to be one way or another, or you feel the need to understand "more fully." *Reflection begins when you admit ignorance and seek knowledge.*

Step 3:   Address relevant questions

The key to effective reflection is asking and answering relevant questions, as the following sample journal entries demonstrate. Note that the relevant questions are in italics.

Observation: Today I passed a house with a sign advertising psychic services— "Palm readings, Tarot cards, Your future foretold!" The house was in a rundown neighborhood. It occurred to me that all such places I've ever seen are in such neighborhoods. *Is that significant?*

Reflection: *What could a psychic accomplish if she used her powers to better herself?* She'd be able to make a fortune at the racetrack or in the stock market or the lottery and could afford to live in the most exclusive section of town. Psychics who live in poor neighborhoods could be unusually humble, refusing to use their powers for their own personal gain, or charlatans.

Observation: Newspaper advertisement: "Good news! Due to the unprecedented success of our giant end-of-year furniture sale, we have extended it for ten days." Somehow that doesn't sound logical.

Reflection: *Is my first impression accurate? Is there something amiss with this ad?* Let's see ... *If the sale had been such a great success, wouldn't they have sold most or all of the furniture? If so, where are they getting the furniture for the extended period?* It doesn't make sense. Perhaps the truth is that the sale was such a flop that they were left with a store full of merchandise and have to extend the sale if they hope to get rid of it. *If this is the case, why didn't it sell? Are the prices too high? Is the quality too low?*

Observation: I read a magazine article about the violence that sometimes occurs at heavy metal rock concerts. The author said that it's unfair to blame the violence on the musicians or the music, and that human beings are naturally violent. This seems to make sense but I want to examine it more closely to be sure.

Reflection: If violence is due to human nature rather than heavy metal musicians and music, then it should occur just as often at other concerts. *What other kinds of musical events should I consider? How about square dances, polka or bluegrass festivals, Natalie Cole or Tony Bennett concerts, or the opera?* I can't remember ever seeing a newspaper headline that said "Riot Mars Pavarotti Performance" or "Rowdy Polka Contestants Attack Bystanders." *Also, if violence is due to human nature, then shouldn't it be found in all societies and all groups within a society?* Yet incidents of violence are much more common in the United States than in Europe or Asia. And even within the United States, violence is virtually unknown among the Amish. These thoughts force me to revise my first impression of the defense of heavy metal music and musicians. I don't know if they can be blamed for the violence at concerts, but they certainly can't be ruled out so conveniently.

Note that the three reflections exhibit imaginativeness. In the first case, the author moved from the observed context—psychic services being offered to others—to another context entirely—psychic services used for one's self. Imagining the new context led to the key thought, "Why don't they pick the winning horse, stock, or lottery numbers?"

In the second case, the author imagined how a store would look after a successful furniture sale—depleted of stock, perhaps even empty. In the third case, the author's imaginativeness was even more impressive, producing general categories of musical events, then specific examples, newspaper headlines, comparisons with Europe and Asia, as well as the example of the Amish.

In all three cases, imagination was stimulated by asking provocative questions. Use this approach to stimulate your imagination.

What about situations in which you don't have all the information you need to make a judgment? In those instances you will have to interrupt your reflection until you have obtained the information. Librarians can direct you to general and special encyclopedias, as well as to articles, books, nonprint materials, and knowledgeable people. And the Internet contains a wealth of information on virtually any topic.

Practicing Critical Thinking 1

Following are a sample observation and a suggestion for reflection. Read both carefully and carry out the suggestion.

Observation

While reading an essay, you encounter this statement: "Each individual creates his or her own morality. The moment a person decides that a behavior is acceptable, it becomes acceptable for that person and no one else has any business criticizing the behavior."

Reflection

Suggestion for reflection: Think of a variety of situations in which a person might decide that a particular behavior is acceptable. For example, a guest at a hotel might think "I paid a lot for this room—I'm entitled to take the towels." Decide whether in those situations the statement in the essay makes sense.

_____

_____

_____

_____

_____

_____

_____

_____

_____

_____

_____

_____

_____

_____

_____

_____

_____

_____

_____

_____

_____

Practicing Critical Thinking 2

Consider the following observation and suggestion for reflection. (Later Practicing Critical Thinking activities will give you progressively less assistance.)

Observation

You hear someone say, "I'm fascinated with the future because the future is where we're going to spend the rest of our lives."

Reflection

*Suggestion for reflection: State and explain your answers to these questions—*Have you ever visited the future? For that matter, have you ever visited the past? Or has your life been a series of present moments? Is this pattern likely to change tomorrow or next year? *Then decide whether the statement about spending the rest of our lives in the future is a reasonable one.*

Practicing Critical Thinking 3

Following are a sample observation and a suggestion for reflection. Read both carefully and carry out the suggestion.

Observation

Line from a television commercial for a used car sales agency: "We'll cosign your loan even if you've had a bankruptcy. That's because we take the trouble to hand pick and inspect these cars before you even see them. . . . We guarantee financing because we only sell quality cars."

Reflection

Suggestion for reflection: Ask yourself this question—How can careful inspection of the car ensure that the buyer of the car will be a good credit risk? In light of your answer, decide whether the statement on the television commercial makes any sense.

_____

_____

_____

_____

_____

_____

_____

_____

_____

_____

_____

_____

_____

_____

_____

_____

_____

_____

_____

_____

_____

_____

_____

Practicing Critical Thinking 4

Following are a sample observation and a suggestion for reflection. Read both carefully and carry out the suggestion.

Observation

A guest on a self-help radio program makes the following statement: "In my counseling practice, I advise my clients to replace all their negative thoughts with positive ones. In other words, if they think 'I'm impatient,' they should say, 'No, I'm patient.' 'I'm clumsy' becomes 'I'm graceful,' and 'I'm a poor athlete' becomes 'I'm an excellent athlete.' I tell them that whatever they believe themselves to be, they will be."

Reflection

Suggestion for reflection: Are there any situations in which people believe they have a quality or skill and they really don't? If you can think of any such situations, list them. Then explain whether the statement "whatever they believe themselves to be, they will be" is reasonable.

_____

_____

_____

_____

_____

_____

_____

_____

_____

_____

_____

_____

_____

_____

_____

_____

_____

_____

_____

_____

_____

_____

_____

_____

Practicing Critical Thinking 5

Following are a sample observation and a suggestion for reflection. Read both carefully and carry out the suggestion.

Observation

When Budweiser Dry beer was introduced, a series of television commercials appeared on the theme "Why ask why? Try Bud Dry." The structure of the ad was to raise a few questions, such as "The Mona Lisa has no eyebrows. Why?" and "Chickens have no lips. Why?" and then to recite the slogan, "Why ask why? Try Bud Dry."

Reflection

Suggestion for reflection: Consider whether this series of commercials encouraged or discouraged curiosity and independent judgment. State and explain your thinking.

_____

_____

_____

_____

_____

_____

_____

_____

_____

_____

_____

_____

_____

_____

Practicing Critical Thinking 6

List as many observations as you can for each of the following categories. Use a separate sheet of paper and save your responses for a later assignment.

a) Interesting issues you would like to address when you have more time

b) Statements that appear to be unusually insightful (they may have been made by authors, instructors, fellow students, or someone else)

c) Statements that seem shallow or mistaken

d) Anything you have experienced or heard about that you wish to understand more fully such as an incident, a process, or a procedure

Quiz

1 This book focuses on evaluating ideas and also includes some approaches for producing them. True or False? Explain.

2 Why is critical thinking an important skill to develop?

3 Explain the error in this statement: "I create my own truth. What I believe to be true is true for me."

4 State the principle of contradiction. Then explain how this statement helps in critical thinking.

5 How can you help your readers in each of the following cases?

a) You are making a statement that you know to be factual but not easily verifiable.

b) You are making a statement that you are not certain is factual.

c) You are making a statement others might disagree with.

6 Is it useful to argue about matters of taste? Explain.

7 Respond to this statement: "I have a right to my opinion, so you have no business challenging it."

8 Define the term *evidence* and give examples of it.

9 Do critical thinkers have convictions? Explain.

10 State and briefly explain the three steps of the comprehensive thinking strategy presented in this chapter.

Answers to this quiz may be found at http://college.hmco.com.

2

Becoming an Individual

Understand individuality

A common meaning of individuality is "uniqueness," a quality that sets a person apart from others. Even so, few people agree about when and how a person becomes an individual.

The popular notion is that we are all individuals from conception and anything we think, say, or do expresses our individuality. Examine this idea to see if it makes sense. If everyone were unique, imitation would be rare. Indeed, it might not exist at all. We'd find little similarity in dress, speech patterns, and mannerisms, let alone viewpoints.

Yet even a casual glance at people reveals a different picture. Count the number of young men's feet in unlaced hightop sneakers. Tally the number of designer labels on male or female behinds. Notice how many businessmen wear suits, shirts, and ties in the current style. See how many businesswomen have hemlines precisely where this year's fashion experts declared they should be.

Note speech patterns, observe mannerisms, listen to viewpoints on issues from abortion and capital punishment to taxation and welfarism. You're likely to see much more sameness than difference.

Such observations suggest that the popular notion of individuality is shallow. People are not born with individuality but with the potential to develop it. Likewise, what people say and do may not express individuality. Actions and words may simply express mindless conformity. Whether someone becomes an individual depends on the effort he or she puts into the task.

An early step in becoming an individual is to admit that we've been shaped by our culture. There's no shame in this. All of us experience this shaping force. When we were children, we learned from other people. This happened first with our parents and other relatives, later with our teachers and peers. We accepted their explanations. We also adopted their attitudes—often without question.

During that same period, most of us saw thousands of hours of television. Small children have difficulty distinguishing between commercials and program content. So as children we probably viewed the ravings of a used car salesman with the same trust we placed in the weather report. More important, uncritical viewing easily becomes a habit. Perhaps we still have our intellectual guard down whenever we watch television.

Many of the attitudes, values, and ideas we regard as an essential part of ourselves were probably formed before we were mature enough to understand them. Perhaps many seemed so familiar that we never questioned them. These are not pleasant conclusions about ourselves, but they are inescapable.

Once we've admitted that some of our attitudes, values, and ideas are borrowed uncritically from others, we can appreciate the importance of discovering where we got them. What's more, we can decide whether we want to keep them.

This intention is key to becoming and remaining an individual. Your environment will continue to shape you as long as you live, so this process of evaluation will never end.

While doing the exercises in this chapter you may be tempted to pretend that you're not influenced by others. If you give in to this temptation, you fool yourself and miss the opportunity to become the person you'd like to be.

Know your attitudes and values

Attitudes are beliefs that are expressed nonverbally, for example through tone of voice, mannerisms, or actions. We are seldom as aware of our attitudes as we are of our other beliefs. So before we can evaluate them, we must first clarify them.

Consider the attitude "I am more important than other people." People who have this attitude seldom express it directly, yet it is revealed by what they say and do. They may demand kindness, sensitivity, and loyalty from others but not practice these virtues; they break dates whenever they wish but resent their friends doing so; they expect apologies but never offer them.

Attitudes generally come from our environment rather than our genes. Americans raised abroad—say in Nigeria, France, China, or Argentina—are likely to have different attitudes than Americans raised in the United States. The religious, social, and political realities of those countries will influence their perspective, sometimes subtly, sometimes more obviously.

Some people say that the main reason Asian boys and girls excel in school is the positive attitudes they have toward parents, teachers, and learning. Likewise, these people suggest that the main reason many other youngsters do poorly is that they lack these positive attitudes.

At the present time in America, popular culture is influencing attitudes more than ever. As we noted in Chapter One, modern entertainment often presents the idea that truth is created rather than discovered, and that everyone has his or her own truth. Constant repetition of this idea persuades many people that whatever they think must be right, merely because they think it. This can pose a great obstacle to critical thinking.

Values are principles, standards, or qualities considered worthwhile or desirable. We all have many values, even if we never analyze them. Specific values and their order of importance differ from person to person. For some people, integrity is the highest value. Faced with a choice between following their conscience and being highly regarded by their peers, they would choose the former. For other people, no value is higher than what others think of them.

Popular culture affects our values. Several decades ago, most people still opposed sex and violence in the media. Then moviemakers and television writers began to push the limits.

Today "trash" television claims a huge following. Also, the more sordid or bizarre the news story, the more attention it receives. Many of us not only accept but expect—in some cases *crave*—a steady diet of the scandalous and the sensational. Like it or not, our values are powerfully shaped by the culture we live in.

Attitudes and values often program opinions. A person who feels hostile toward minorities is more likely than others to believe the worst when an African American or a Latino receives a promotion. People who strongly value self-reliance might oppose assistance programs for poor people, especially if they feel that poverty is blameworthy. A person who values respect for elders will take the problem of rudeness more seriously than others do.

> There are times when the greatest change needed is a change of my viewpoint.
>
> —C. M. Ward

Like attitudes, values affect the quality of our thinking. If we value consistency more highly than truth, we will hesitate to change our minds, even when sound reasoning calls on us to do so. If we assign our feelings a higher priority than evidence, the quality of our reasoning is likely to suffer.

One crucial step to becoming a critical thinker is evaluating your attitudes and values. The purpose of the following exercises is to help you with that evaluation. These exercises work best if you respond directly and honestly. *Don't screen out any ideas or change them to fit what you think others might want you to say.* If you turn in these exercises, be sure to save them when your instructor returns them to you. Later exercises will build on what you write here.

Exercise 11

A. Record your first thought on each of the following subjects in the space provided. (Be sure to say what comes to mind and not what you think you are supposed to say.)

Keeping promises

_____

_____

_____

Being on time

_____

_____

_____

Good manners

_____

_____

_____

Personal appearance

_____

_____

_____

Success in life

_____

_____

_____

Authority of teachers, parents, employers, and others

_____

_____

_____

Discipline

_____

_____

_____

Apologizing

_____

_____

_____

Excellence

_____

_____

_____

B. Now evaluate what you recorded in Part A. In each case decide whether your reaction is positive, constructive, and beneficial. If it is not, explain what reaction would be better.

_____

_____

_____

_____

_____

_____

_____

_____

_____

_____

_____

_____

_____

_____

_____

_____

_____

_____

_____

_____

_____

Know your mental habits

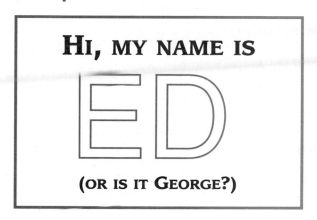

HI, MY NAME IS

ED

(OR IS IT GEORGE?)

You're at a party and notice several people standing near you. One of them says, "Betty, meet George." You're shocked. That guy's name isn't George, you think. It's Ed. Later, you seek out the person who made the introduction and ask him if he made a mistake. He assures you he didn't.

As the evening wears on, you hear other people saying "George" this and "George" that. You reflect on the dozens, hundreds of times you've called him Ed. Apparently he was too polite to correct you. Your face flushes with embarrassment at the thought. "How could I have been so dumb?" you say over and over to yourself.

It's not a matter of being dumb. In fact, it has very little to do with intelligence. The real cause is the bad habit of taking first impressions for granted and ignoring experiences that challenge them.

I know people who never missed an episode of the popular Seinfeld show. Yet they continued to mispronounce the star's name, calling him "Steinfeld." Similarly, countless congressmen, journalists, and military officers mispronounce the word *nuclear*. They say "nu-*kew*-lar" instead of "nu-*clee*-ar."

Another bad mental habit is judging on the basis of personal likes and dislikes rather than on evidence. People who have this habit accept rumors about people they dislike and reject negative facts about people they like.

A third bad mental habit is refusing to accept responsibility for one's own bad choices. People who have this habit fool themselves into believing that whatever goes wrong in their lives is someone else's fault. (When things go right, of course, they are quick to claim credit.)

The first step in developing new and better mental habits is to make an honest assessment of your existing habits. The following exercises will help you do that.

Exercise 12

Read the following statements one at a time. Notice what happens as you read them and immediately afterward. Perhaps you'll hear the words or see them in your mind. It might seem as if they're on a screen, with one word more clearly in focus than the others. Perhaps you'll produce a vivid mental picture. Or perhaps you'll move quickly to some association or experience. A happy, say, or an angry feeling might rise up in you. These responses are clues to your mental habits.

Here's a useful strategy for this assignment. Write your immediate response to the statement. Expand that response if you can. Then look back at what you've written and describe the process of thinking or feeling as it unfolded.

Consider the following example.

A sample statement:

Trend is not destiny. —Lewis Mumford

An immediate response:
Trend *means the way a person or many people are heading or behaving.* Destiny *is what a person and his or her life are meant to be. So what does this statement mean? That my thoughts and actions aren't the only possible ones, even if they feel as if they are. I can choose against the force of habit or peer pressure. For example, I don't have to wear the "in" clothes or agree with the most popular ideas. I can assert my individuality. Mumford's idea makes sense to me.*

An analysis of the immediate response:
In this case my first reaction was to go over in my mind what the key words of the sentence mean. Then I restated the sentence to recapture its full meaning. Next came to mind an example of how the idea applies in my life. Finally, I decided I agreed with it.

Success is a journey, not a destination. —Ben Sweetland

_____

_____

_____

_____

Many people's tombstones should read "Died at 30. Buried at 60." —Nicholas Murray Butler

_____

_____

_____

_____

Women should remain at home, sit still, keep house, and bear and bring up children.
—Martin Luther

_____

_____

_____

_____

Victory has a hundred fathers, but defeat is an orphan. —Count G. Ciano

_____

_____

_____

_____

I do not believe in the collective wisdom of individual ignorance. —Thomas Carlyle

_____

_____

_____

_____

Exercise 13

Describe your reactions to the following situations, as you did in Exercise 12. Include your typical feelings, thoughts, words, and actions.

a) *You express a point of view in a conversation and a friend disagrees with you.*

_____

_____

_____

_____

b) *You're in a large class and the teacher calls on you.*

_____

_____

_____

_____

c) *You're doing a homework assignment and are unsure how to proceed.*

_____

_____

_____

d) *You're listening to someone you don't like. He's talking to a group of your friends, and they seem interested in what he's saying.*

_____

_____

_____

_____

e) *You begin reading a book or an article on a subject you feel strongly about. Then you realize the author's view strongly opposes yours.*

_____

_____

_____

_____

Exercise 14

List (1) the books, magazines, and newspapers you most enjoy reading, (2) the courses of study that most interest you, and (3) the web sites you most often visit. Explain what you find attractive about each.

_____

_____

_____

_____

_____

_____

_____

_____

_____

_____

_____

_____

_____

_____

_____

_____

Exercise 15

While doing a reading assignment for one of your courses, answer these questions:

■   *What is your typical way of approaching such an assignment? Do you plunge right in or skim it first? If you skim, what specifically do you look for?*

_____

_____

_____

_____

■   *How long can you maintain your attention before you're distracted?*

_____

_____

_____

_____

■   *What kinds of distractions bother you more—external distractions or those in your own mind?*

_____

_____

_____

_____

Exercise 16

What is your characteristic response to problems and controversial issues? Do you tend to react emotionally or rationally? In what situations do you tend to be at your best? At your worst? What about those situations influences your reaction?

_____

_____

_____

_____

_____

_____

_____

Exercise 17

Have you ever made any statements like the following? If so, describe when and where you made each statement. Identify the mental habit associated with your reaction.

"This course doesn't matter because it's not required for my major."

_____

_____

_____

"This instructor is assigning too much work."

_____

_____

_____

"It's only fair for the instructor to put something on the test if she said we were responsible for knowing it."

_____

_____

_____

"If the class gets too tough, I'll drop it."

_____

_____

_____

"The reason I'm doing poorly is that the teacher doesn't like me."

_____

_____

_____

"Students who take part in class discussions are just trying to impress the teacher."

_____

_____

_____

Practice critical thinking behaviors

Critical thinkers differ from other people in a number of ways. The first sections of this chapter helped you develop one of them: self-knowledge. Philosophy is said to have begun in the directive "Know thyself." The wisdom of that directive has remained strong over the 2,500 years since Socrates first expressed it. Knowing your own mind is one step in using it effectively.

Critical thinkers are uncommon in other ways, too. By understanding the qualities of such individuals you can learn to think more effectively. Following are some important qualities. Begin practicing them today.

Critical thinkers are honest with themselves

Through uncritical thinking, people deceive themselves. They pretend that the truth is what they wish it to be. They persuade themselves that they can drive 30 miles per hour over the speed limit without endangering themselves or others. They think drinking a six-pack of beer each day is no signal of a drinking problem, or that missing class has no effect on grades. They believe that hotel managers expect guests to steal towels, and that copying computer programs is morally acceptable. When someone disagrees, they dismiss the challenge immediately.

Critical thinkers avoid such self-deception. They acknowledge even unpleasant ideas. If they do something foolish or immoral, they refuse to compound the mistake by pretending it was sensible or moral. When they hear a valid argument, they accept it—even if that means rejecting a cherished personal view.

Critical thinkers' honesty with themselves comes from admitting their limits. They know that to be human is to be fallible. They know that "knowledge" in most cases is an assortment of facts, assumptions, interpretations, and conclusions. So they are cautious about claiming certainty.

This perspective is not popular today. We are told we should be confident, trust our judgment completely, and assert our views without reservation. Intellectual humility is often considered a handicap. This idea can lead many people to express opinions on matters they know little or nothing about.

Critical thinkers resist the temptation to feign knowledge. They realize that admitting ignorance opens their minds to learning.

Critical thinkers resist manipulation

The desire to be admired and accepted by others can make us easier to manipulate. Advertisers know it, and they design ads to play on this desire. They promise that lipstick or aftershave will make us irresistible. They also tell us that cars, clothes, or toilet bowl cleaners will make us the envy of the neighborhood.

Three of the most common themes used in the media to manipulate the public are:

1. Self-indulgence. The appeal here is "Don't deny yourself this [product or service]. Go ahead and treat yourself. You deserve it."

2. Impulsiveness. This appeal is "Don't delay. Don't pause to think and evaluate. Just act."

3. Instant gratification. The appeal here is "Why wait? You can enjoy it now and it will make you feel s-o-o-o-o good."

Advertisers aren't the only ones who use these and other forms of manipulation. People who want to sell us their ideas or proposals—such as politicians—often manipulate our thinking rather than use honest persuasion.

Former White House advisor Dick Morris says that today's political speeches are like collections of "greatest hits." The speakers say what polls show the public wants to hear. This explains why words like *trust, family,* and *values* are so often used.

We can defend against manipulation by admitting that we are vulnerable to it and staying alert to detect it.

Critical thinkers overcome confusion

Like everyone else, critical thinkers are sometimes confused. What sets critical thinkers apart is that they don't stay confused. When they can look up something in a reference book or check with an authority, they take the initiative. They find an answer.

Many times all that is needed is more careful thinking. When critical thinkers meet a sentence whose meaning eludes them, they consider a number of possible meanings. Then they choose the most likely one.

Suppose a critical thinker has difficulty understanding the meaning of this proverb: "The girl who can't dance says the band can't play." She wonders, Is the reference here to dancing or to other situations as well? Just how broad is its meaning? Then she considers how the proverb applies to other situations: a small boy having trouble catching the ball and blaming the thrower; a student having trouble with a course and blaming the teacher. Finally, the critical thinker concludes that the proverb covers a wide variety of situations and might be paraphrased "People tend to blame others for their own shortcomings."

Critical thinkers ask questions

Critical thinkers realize that it's easy to make shallow, inaccurate statements. So when they're dealing with ideas, they ask penetrating questions to test the ideas.

Here is a viewpoint, followed by questions a critical thinker might ask. The question numbers correspond to the sentence numbers.

Viewpoint:
(1) I'm disappointed with the instructors at this university—they seem content to offer uninteresting courses. (2) For example, they stand at the lectern and lecture all

period without enthusiasm for their material. (3) On the rare occasions when they open discussion to the class, they call on the same few students. (4) The rest of us have to sit squirming, waiting for the boring ordeal to be over. (5) I wish the faculty at this institution cared enough to make their classes interesting.

Questions:

1. How likely is it that the writer knows all or most of the instructors at this university?

2. How likely is it that all or most of the instructors teach strictly by lecture and without enthusiasm?

3. Why are the same few students always called on (assuming this claim is accurate)? Do these students raise their hands and show an interest in the questions? Do other students, including the writer, ever volunteer a comment or question?

4. Are all but a few students at this university really so bored? Or has the writer projected his reaction on them? Is it possible that the students who squirm have overly negative attitudes?

5. Whose responsibility is it to make a class interesting? The instructor's alone? Do the students bear any responsibility?

Critical thinkers take the time to produce many ideas

Many people are idea-poor. For each challenge that confronts them they have a single answer, often the first one that pops into their minds or one they see in print or hear on television. With that approach, the odds of their producing insightful ideas are slender.

When the price of a postage stamp was increased by three cents, people with a supply of the older stamps had to combine them with three-cent stamps to make the correct postage. The lines at post offices in some areas were unusually long, and the demand for three-cent stamps quickly exceeded the supply. One reason was that some people bought many more stamps than they needed. For example, people who needed 10 three-cent stamps bought 50 or 100. Perhaps they believed the stamps would increase in value.

It got even sillier. One man entering a post office saw the sign "Sorry, we're temporarily out of three-cent stamps." He grumbled in displeasure and said as he walked away, "I've driven to four post offices and they're all out of stamps. Now I've got to try a fifth." Apparently he never considered other options. He could have walked up to the window, bought some four-cent stamps—plenty were available—and mailed his letters.

To avoid such embarrassing mistakes, produce lots of ideas before embracing any one. Extend your effort to identify possibilities. A helpful technique is **springboarding**. Here's how it works: Think of an idea and add to it right away. Resist the urge to dwell on details. Don't worry about writing complete sentences; a word or short phrase will do. Use one idea to propel you to others. To keep the process going, end each item in your list with the word *and*.

Say that the subject you are addressing is students' attitudes in class. Your list of ideas might be as follows. Note how asking questions cues you to continue springboarding. The cue questions below are italicized.

Attitudes in Class

What Attitudes?

disinterest in class and

hostility to the teacher and . . .

Are There More?

disapproval of students who speak and

uncooperativeness in class discussion and

disrespect for other students and . . .

How Are Attitudes Revealed?

smirking and

whispering while others are talking and

arriving late for class and

making rude remarks and

doing unrelated things like cleaning nails, and . . .

Why Do Students Do These Things?

to maintain a "tough" image and

to hide fear of failing and

to make teachers uncomfortable and . . .

What Are Some Favorable Attitudes?

cooperativeness and

willingness to listen to others' viewpoints and

patience when the discussion gets complex and . . .

How Are These Attitudes Revealed?

looking at the person speaking and

waiting for her to finish before you speak and

refraining from side discussions and

emphasizing the positive and . . .

The list could go on. You could think about how some students develop positive attitudes and others develop negative ones. Or you might explore how teachers can effectively deal with students who have negative attitudes.

Here is an additional tip: Be open to ideas at all times. You may find that insights occur to you when you don't expect them—while you shower, walk from class to class, or fall asleep at night. Perhaps you said to yourself on some of these occasions, "I've got to remember this idea later," and found later that you had forgotten it.

To capture ideas, as noted in the introduction, keep a pen and paper handy. That way you can record ideas when they occur. Once you start doing so, chances are you'll be rewarded with many more ideas.

Critical thinkers base their judgments on evidence

Many people pay little attention to the need for evidence. In fact, they often form their views first and seek support for them later. Critical thinkers weigh the evidence before making a judgment. And if they have a bias toward a particular view, they make a special effort to be fair minded.

Critical thinkers are sensitive to the need for evidence. They seek it out and resolve any conflicts in it. They also make sure it is sufficient in kind and quantity to permit a conclusion.

Critical thinkers acknowledge complexity

Critical thinkers know that in controversial issues the truth is often complex. They make judgments reflecting that complexity. For example, ask several people, "Do you think today's politicians are honest?" You may hear one of the following replies:

> *"They're crooks, obviously, hypocrites, the lot of them."*
> *"All politicians disgust me."*

Critical thinkers recognize that neither of these answers does justice to the question. They're more likely to say, *"Some politicians are dishonest. Still, there are likely many honest, dedicated politicians as well. I try to consider each person separately."*

Critical thinkers are not mechanical in their thinking. Being human, they experience the same emotional reactions and temptations to snap judgment and overstatement as anyone else. Yet critical thinkers make a conscious effort to control those reactions and avoid those temptations. Before they express a view they take the trouble to be sure it is responsibly formed.

Critical thinkers look for connections between subjects

Schools, colleges, and universities have English departments, history departments, chemistry departments, and so on. Over the centuries, educators found it convenient to organize knowledge that way. Unfortunately, some people assume that all subjects fall into neat compartments. These people don't try to connect one subject with another. That notion prevents them from becoming critical thinkers.

Critical thinkers realize that concepts and strategies learned in one subject often apply to other subjects. What's more, they know that most serious problems touch many fields. AIDS, for example, creates not only medical challenges but psychological, legal, and moral challenges as well.

Critical thinkers are intellectually independent

To many people, intellectual independence means, "I'll do everything my own way. I'll ignore what others think and do." This perspective hinders learning and is self-defeating. Life is too short for learning all we need to know solely through our own experiences. Ideas from others can make us dependent only if we accept them without thinking.

Critical thinkers realize this and are eager to learn from others' experiences. They seek out and consider a wide spectrum of ideas on important issues. Then they make their own judgments. Critical thinkers also reassess views when new evidence comes to light. Each of these habits promotes genuine intellectual independence.

Exercise 18

Think of a time when you pretended that you knew something that in fact you did not know. Would you have gained by being more honest about your ignorance? If so, in what way?

_____

_____

_____

_____

_____

_____

_____

_____

_____

_____

_____

Exercise 19

Think of an occasion when you were manipulated. Describe how it happened. Explain specific steps you can take to avoid being manipulated in the future.

_____
_____
_____
_____
_____
_____
_____
_____
_____
_____
_____
_____
_____

Exercise 20

Give one or more examples of advertisements that use the following themes:

Self-indulgence ("Don't deny yourself")

_____
_____
_____
_____
_____
_____
_____
_____

Impulsiveness ("Don't think—just act")

_____

_____

_____

_____

_____

_____

_____

_____

Instant gratification ("Experience pleasure now")

_____

_____

_____

_____

_____

_____

_____

_____

Exercise 21

Explain in your own words what each of the following sayings means. If you aren't sure of the meaning, overcome your confusion by identifying possible meanings and deciding which is most plausible.

A cathedral, a wave of a storm, a dancer's leap, never turn out to be as high as we had hoped. —Marcel Proust

_____

_____

_____

_____

_____

_____

_____

Happiness is not a state to arrive at, but a manner of traveling. —Margaret Lee Runbeck

_____

_____

_____

_____

_____

_____

_____

Men are not punished for their sins, but by them. —Elbert G. Hubbard

_____

_____

_____

_____

_____

_____

_____

Exercise 22

Consider each of the following statements. Decide whether each is completely true, partly true, or completely false. Don't just accept your first reactions; decide if those reactions are reasonable. If you find any statement partly true, explain in what way it's true and in what way it is not.

Never has a man who has bent himself been able to make others straight. —Mencius

_____

_____

_____

_____

_____

Free will does not mean one will, but many wills in one [person]. —Flannery O'Connor

_____

_____

_____

_____

_____

_____

_____

_____

_____

_____

The offender never forgives. —Russian proverb

_____

_____

_____

_____

_____

_____

_____

_____

_____

_____

No matter which side of an argument you're on, you always find some people on your side that you wish were on the other side. —Jascha Heifetz

_____

_____

_____

_____

_____

_____

_____

_____

_____

_____

Be constructive in discussions

Collaborative effort plays an important role in business and the professions. In your career you will likely be expected to work harmoniously with other people. Often those people will be from different cultural backgrounds and have different areas of specialization and viewpoints.

In other words, you will be challenged to use your critical thinking in groups as well as individually. Class discussion is the best training ground for this skill.

Many people have a mistaken notion about class discussion and of group activity in general. Some view discussion as competition, with one winner and many losers. As a result, they approach it combatively. They interrupt, shout, and browbeat others into submission.

Others view discussion as serial monologue, with every person taking a turn at speaking but no one listening to anyone else.

Neither type of person is an asset to group activity.

At its best, group discussion is an opportunity to share, test ideas, and create meaning. But this opportunity is possible only in a context of cooperation. In this context, participants approach discussion eager to listen as well as to speak, and they are prepared to explore all views vigorously yet fairly without anger or resentment. They adopt the group's goal as their own personal goal.

The following guidelines will help you become a constructive contributor. Practicing them now will help you in years to come.

1. Prepare for discussions   If the discussion is scheduled in advance, spend some time planning for it. Study the lesson or meeting agenda, considering each point to be discussed. When a problem or an issue is involved, apply your thinking skills to it and be prepared to share your thoughts with others.

2. Anticipate disputes   When people of different backgrounds and perspectives address issues, disputes often arise. These can be beneficial to the group, as long as they are approached constructively. The key is to detach your ego from your ideas.

Regard your ideas as tentative and the meeting as an opportunity to modify and improve them. Expect others to disagree with you and criticize your view. Refuse to take criticism personally.

3. Leave private agendas outside   From time to time you may find yourself working in a group with someone you don't care for. You may have had trouble with the person in a past meeting or your personalities may just clash. Dislike for the person may tempt you to be disagreeable and even sarcastic.

Such reactions hinder the group's efforts and make meetings unpleasant for everyone. You have an obligation to the group to give your best, so refuse to let your feelings toward anyone influence your behavior or your response to his or her ideas.

4. Cooperate with the leader   Keep in mind that the group leader has special obligations such as moving efficiently through the meeting's agenda, maintaining order, keeping discussion positive, and ensuring that all members are heard from and all perspectives considered. When the leader attempts to meet those obligations, be understanding and cooperative.

5. Listen to others   When another group member has the floor, look at that person and be attentive, whether you agree or disagree. Don't permit yourself to be distracted by other people or your own thoughts. And avoid doing anything that causes others to be inattentive.

6. Understand before judging   If you are uncertain whether you understand a particular view, ask the person who expressed it. For example, say, "Ann, I'm not sure I heard you correctly. Are you saying that . . . ?" Then listen carefully to her answer. Base your evaluation on what she said rather than on careless assumptions about what she meant.

7. Be balanced   Many of the views expressed in discussion are of mixed quality. That is, they are partly valid and partly invalid, somewhat wise and somewhat foolish. Thus, the most reasonable response will often be to agree in part rather than to agree completely or disagree completely. To be sure your evaluation is fair, take special care to find the flaws in views you agree with and the merits of views you disagree with.

8. Be courteous   When views clash and discussions grow heated, it's easy to forget the rules of civility. When that happens, bad feelings usually follow and group accomplishments are threatened. To avoid such outcomes, make it your habit to give no offense to others and to be slow to take offense yourself.

9. Monitor your contributions   Be aware of how often you contribute to the discussion. If you tend to speak a lot, make an effort to limit your contributions to matters you regard as important. On the other hand, if you seldom say anything, start contributing more often. (If others express your ideas before you get a chance to, you can always express agreement and explain your reasons.)

Also monitor the *kinds* of contributions that you make to discussions. Ideally, you will propose ideas of your own *and* offer constructive criticism of other people's ideas. If all your contributions are criticisms, you will be a hindrance rather than a help to the group.

10. Be alert for insights   When knowledgeable people exchange ideas, they often stimulate one another's thinking and produce new insights. Unfortunately, insights are often so mixed in with ordinary ideas that they go unnoticed. You will be better able to find them if you actively look for them in all contributions, other people's as well as your own.

Present your ideas to advantage

When you express an idea, would you rather that people accept it or reject it? You may be thinking, "What a silly question. Of course I would rather have people accept what I say. Wouldn't everyone?"

Everyone may prefer acceptance to rejection, but many do little or nothing to make that preference a reality. In fact, many people are so careless that they *invite rejection.*

By advoiding their mistakes, you can increase your chance of getting a favorable reaction for your ideas.

Mistake 1: Hurried or careless thinking

People who commit this error rush the thinking process. They trust their first impressions instead of testing them. They rely exclusively on their own personal experience rather than consulting many sources of information. They ignore complexity instead of acknowledging it. As a result of these habits, their ideas are usually shallow and difficult to defend.

Mistake 2: Careless expression

Some people don't even try to express their ideas well. They assume their listeners or readers will struggle to find their message, however buried it may be in vague, clumsy wording.

Guess what? Those people are kidding themselves. Most listeners and readers reason that if the speaker or writer won't bother to express the idea carefully, the idea probably isn't worth very much.

Mistake 3: Foolish expectation

Many people expect that others are eager to hear their ideas and ready to accept them uncritically. In reality, everyone has his or her own ideas and is quick to question opposing ones.

Note: Chapter Seven, "Expressing Ideas Persuasively," offers additional advice on how to present your ideas to advantage. Feel free to look ahead to it.

Exercise 23

Read each of the following viewpoints carefully. Then write pertinent questions in the spaces provided.

Viewpoint 1:
(1) Some people believe that professional wrestling should be seen as an entertainment rather than a sport. I disagree. (2) Professional wrestling demands athletic skill. (3) It involves competition so intense that it often results in physical injury. (4) I admit it is entertaining, but so are football, boxing, and tennis. (5) If the critics dared to enter the ring with a professional wrestler, they'd quickly learn that wrestling is not mere entertainment.

_____

_____

_____

_____

_____

_____

_____

_____

_____

Viewpoint 2:
(1) Far from being harmful, reading pornographic literature or watching pornographic films is healthy. (2) Such material helps young people learn about sex. (3) It provides enjoyment to millions of men and an increasing number of women. (4) And it helps to break down the puritanism that has caused our rising divorce rate.

_____

_____

_____

_____

_____

_____

_____

_____

Exercise 24

On a separate sheet of paper answer each of the following questions and add your reasons for thinking as you do. Then ask pertinent questions about what you have written. (Be sure to be as critical of these viewpoints as you are of other people's.)

a) Can animals think?
b) Should gambling be legalized?
c) Should teachers be allowed to spank elementary school children who misbehave in school?
d) Do smokers tend to discount the evidence that smoking can kill them?
e) Should the government assume control of the Internet, deciding who can have access and under what conditions?

Now select one of these issues for further examination. Answer the questions you raised about your viewpoint by doing research on the Internet, in the library, or through interviews. Record your findings.

Exercise 25

Select one of the following topics and research it on the Internet, in the library, and/or through interviews. State the different views you encounter. Then explain which view is best supported by the evidence.

a) Is it wrong to criticize another person's view of a controversial issue?
b) Is it acceptable to subject animals to painful experiments in order to find cures for diseases?
c) Is it possible for atheists to be as moral as religious believers?

Practicing Critical Thinking 7

In Chapter One, Practicing Critical Thinking 6, you made some observations and were asked to save them for closer examination at a later time. Now is the time.

Select one of the observations you made and restate it below. Then reflect on it by asking and answering relevant questions.

_____

_____

_____

_____

_____

_____

_____

_____

_____

_____

_____

_____

_____

_____

Practicing Critical Thinking 8

You have probably made many observations in each of the following categories since those you recorded in Practicing Critical Thinking 6 in Chapter One. List these more recent observations on a separate sheet of paper and save them for a later assignment.
a) Interesting issues you would like to address when you have more time
b) Statements that appear to be unusually insightful (they may have been made by authors, instructors, fellow students, or someone else)
c) Statements that seem to be shallow or mistaken
d) Anything you have experienced or heard about that you wish to understand more fully such as an incident, a process, or a procedure

Quiz

1 Write your viewpoint on this statement: "Everyone is born an individual and everything a person says or does is an expression of his or her uniqueness." Offer evidence to support your viewpoint.

2 What is the first step in becoming an individual as explained in this chapter?

3 According to this chapter, what is the key to becoming and remaining an individual?

4 What are attitudes and how do we get them?

5 What are values?

6 Do people's values affect the quality of their thinking? Explain your answer.

7 According to this chapter, much of what is regarded as intellectual excellence is a matter of having good mental habits. True or False? Explain.

8 This chapter discussed several characteristics of critical thinkers. One of them is self-knowledge. List the others.

9 List four ways to be constructive in discussions.

Answers to this quiz may be found at http://college.hmco.com.

3

Evaluating
Arguments

What is argument?

The word *argument* is sometimes used in the sense of "quarrel"—that is, a dispute characterized by angry exchanges. That is not the use intended here. We will use the term as philosophers do, to mean presenting a point of view about an issue.

When you read about opinion and evidence in Chapter One, you were dealing with the essential ingredients of argument—what you think about something and why you think it. Now we'll consider the more detailed kind of argument found in formal writing.

Argument aims to get other people to accept a particular viewpoint. Candidates for political office argue when they present their positions on issues. Lawyers argue when they try cases in court.

Argument's focus on persuasion distinguishes it from news reporting, which merely provides information. (Journalists have traditionally been advised to confine their personal views to the editorial or "opinion page.")

An argument may be as short as a single sentence or as long as an article or even a book. Nevertheless, whatever its length, an argument expresses a line of reasoning.

It may be helpful to think of an argument as a kind of equation, such as *a* plus *b* equals *c*. Whether the argument is sound or unsound depends on what is actually said in the equation. "Twenty plus seventy equals ninety" is sound. On the other hand, "Thirteen plus fourteen equals thirty" is unsound. So is "Roses are red; Irish setters are red; therefore, Irish setters are roses."

Logic offers numerous rules for deciding whether an argument passes the test of critical thinking. Those rules are beyond the scope of this book. We will focus on the most fundamental criterion:

> *An argument passes the test of critical thinking when it is shown to be more reasonable than competing arguments and better supported by the evidence.*

What is evidence?

As noted in Chapter One, evidence is anything that supports a claim or assertion. The most common and obvious kind of evidence is an example or case in point. Suppose someone says, "Telephone solicitors can be very rude" and proceeds to describe a recent experience she had with a caller. The example "backs up" her assertion.

Of course, if the claim were more sweeping, such as "Telephone solicitors are *usually* rude," more than a single example would be needed. The person making the claim would be challenged to show that the rudeness she encountered was *typical* of telephone solicitors.

When the occasion is more formal and the issue is more serious, other kinds of evidence are appropriate. We will examine eight kinds. Each has specific strengths and weaknesses.

Published reports are found in newspapers, broadcasts, books, magazines, and the Internet. This is the most common kind of evidence and the *least* reliable. Careless and dishonorable reporters allow their biases to influence their reporting. And even conscientious reporters can make mistakes. The chance for error is especially great when the information is acquired in haste or from second- or third-hand accounts. Never assume that a report is accurate just because it appears in print or is broadcast.

Eyewitness testimony is a report of what someone observed first-hand. It may be reliable, but can easily be influenced by preconceived notions. As someone once noted, "People don't just believe what they see. Sometimes *they see what they believe*." Also, the memory of one event can be distorted by subsequent events. Question eyewitness testimony before accepting it.

Expert opinions are statements made by authorities. They are generally more reliable than the opinions of non-experts. Yet experts often disagree, and even when they agree, they can be mistaken. (Knowledge is exploding in every field. A person can have the right credentials and the best intentions and yet fail to keep up with developments.) Thus it is unwise to settle for experts' *statements* alone. Look also for the data on which the opinions are based.

Experiments are of two types. The field experiment has the advantage of occurring in a natural setting; the laboratory experiment is more controlled and thus more precise. A good test of whether an experiment is reliable is successful repetition by another, independent researcher.

Statistics usually refers to quantitative information obtained about every individual in a group or category. Examples of statistics are the percentage of deaths caused by drunken driving, the comparative college admissions scores of various racial and ethnic groups, and the voting records of members of Congress. If the statistical sources are reputable, the statistics will generally be trustworthy. But it is prudent to check that they are quoted accurately.

Surveys obtain data by taking a scientific sample of the members of a group. A sample can be reliable even though a very small number of individuals were contacted, but only if certain conditions were met. All members of the group must have had an equal chance of being contacted. Also, the questions must have been clear, unambiguous, and unbiased. Keep in mind that the way survey questions are phrased can influence the responses.

Formal observation involves watching a group of people go about their everyday activities. For example, one might observe a group of children at play, participants at a political convention, or Amish farmers raising a barn. For the results of the observation to be reliable, the observer must not have influenced the behavior of the group. Also, the period of observation must have been of reasonable duration.

Research reviews examine the general body of research information on a topic. It is not uncommon for such a review to cover dozens, even hundreds, of independent research studies. A research review is a highly reliable form of evidence if it covers all significant research studies and is free of bias.

The rest of the chapter will examine the steps to take in evaluating an argument:

Step 1: Understand the argument

Step 2: Seek out competing views

Step 3: Sort out disagreements

Step 4: Make your judgment

STEP 1: Understand the argument

Brief arguments are often easily understood. Longer, more detailed arguments pose a greater challenge. In such cases, see the argument as a piece of fabric with many single strands of thought woven together. Closely examine the weave to reveal the individual strands.

Skim for the main idea

To begin, skim the article or book and find the main idea. This idea is usually stated in or immediately after the introduction and is reinforced in the conclusion. The introduction may vary in length. In a brief article it may be half a paragraph; in a longer article, a paragraph or two; in a book, an entire chapter.

Identifying the main idea is your key to understanding the writer's argument. The writer's choices—what evidence to include, how to arrange it, what objections to address—are made with that idea in mind. If you take time to find the main idea before reading the entire article, reading can be faster and more effective.

Read with the main idea in mind

After skimming the article or book and finding the main idea, read the article or book with the main idea in mind. Distinguish between assertions and evidence. A typical pattern of writers is to make an assertion and then support it with explanation, factual details, examples, and so on. Writers who support their assertions will often include several sentences of support for every sentence of assertion. Not all writers do this, however.

When possible, read the entire article or book in a single sitting. You may find your grasp of the writer's argument improves. To read more efficiently, postpone looking up the definitions of words until later. Of course, if you do not understand a word in the main idea or some other key word, look it up immediately.

Identify evidence

When you finish reading the article or book, look back over it and identify the evidence offered in support of the main idea. Knowing basic relationships between the parts of an argument can help you find evidence quickly and accurately.

"And" relationships signal that what follows adds to what preceded. For example, they may signal that more evidence is being offered to support an assertion. Words used for "and" relationships include *also, first (second,* and so on); *in addition, next, further, and, moreover, finally, lastly, besides,* and *another.*

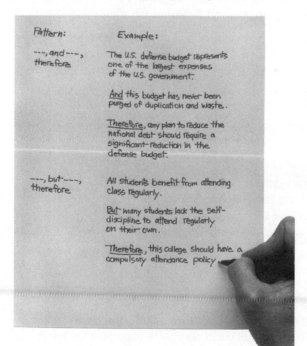

Pattern:

---, and ---, therefore

Example:

The U.S. defense budget represents one of the largest expenses of the U.S. government.

And this budget has never been purged of duplication and waste.

Therefore, any plan to reduce the national debt should require a significant reduction in the defense budget.

---, but ---, therefore

All students benefit from attending class regularly.

But many students lack the self-discipline to attend regularly on their own.

Therefore, this college should have a compulsory attendance policy.

"But" relationships signal that what follows contrasts with what preceded. What follows is usually an exception or qualification. Words used to signal "but" relationships include *however, nevertheless, yet, or, but, on the other hand,* and *in contrast.*

"Therefore" relationships signal that a conclusion follows from the preceding evidence. Words used to signal "therefore" relationships include *so, consequently, accordingly, thus, therefore,* and *it follows that.*

The illustration shows the most typical patterns of relationships you'll encounter in persuasive writing and speaking.

Longer articles and books will include a series of these relationships. One example: _____, and _____, and _____, but _____, and _____, therefore _____. (The material represented by each line may comprise a sentence, a paragraph, or a chapter.)

High school English teachers might have discouraged you from using *and* or *but* to begin a sentence. But that prohibition has no basis. Even a quick scanning of enduring works of literature reveals that writers have long used these words to begin sentences. *Therefore,* feel free to do so in your writing. (Notice that this very paragraph is organized in the _____, but _____, therefore _____ pattern.)

As you gain skill in unraveling arguments, you'll be able to identify relationships while you read. For now, treat finding relationships as a separate step.

Summarize

When you have finished reading the article and identifying the evidence offered in support of the main idea, write a summary of the book or article. An effective summary:

- Is written in your own words. Using your words rather than the author's words helps you remember the ideas.

- Emphasizes key points. Authors use the same techniques taught in high school and college writing. They make assertions, develop them, and present examples. In summarizing, record only the assertions and leave out the supporting material.

- Is accurate. Paraphrasing can cause mistakes. Take care that your summary represents the author's view accurately. If the author emphasizes or qualifies a point, reflect this in your summary. If you wish to add your own comments, put them in brackets. Then you can easily identify them as your own later.

Carefully done summaries can really improve your understanding of arguments.

Exercise 26

Analyze the arguments in each of the following articles, following the steps explained in "Step 1: Understand the argument." Write your responses in the spaces provided. Future assignments will build on this one.

The government's role in gambling

The man waits nervously in the long line of people. He's already late for work, and he knows the boss will be angry with him. But he's determined not to leave; he has a strong feeling that this will be the luckiest day of his life. What could possibly be important enough to risk offending one's employer? Buying a ticket on the lottery.

Today's lottery operations and their companion enterprises, off-track betting parlors, are big business. Government officials see them as ideal ways to raise billions of dollars in revenue without raising taxes. The reasoning is that since many people enjoy gambling and no one is hurt by it, there's nothing wrong with the government's taking a piece of the action and using the proceeds to benefit the public.

That reasoning is mistaken. Gambling is a vice. People are hurt by it. It's wrong for the government to be involved in it—every bit as wrong as it would be for the government to run a chain of brothels or a tobacco company or a liquor distillery.

Addiction to gambling is no less a disease than alcoholism. People afflicted by it do not act freely when they place a bet; they are compelled to do so. And they aren't the only ones hurt when they throw away their money: their spouses and children also suffer. Money that could buy food and clothing, pay the rent, or buy dental care is invested in the childish expectation of beating the odds.

The advertisements for the lottery and off-track betting are cleverly crafted to create the impression that the bettor has a good chance of winning. For example, one commercial begins with the words to an old song, "Fairy tales can come true, it can happen to you . . ." and goes on to dramatize the experience of winning. Slogans like "You can't win it if you're not in it" tease bettors to buy a ticket. And the one in ten or twenty million people who happens to win a big jackpot has his or her picture in the paper and is an instant celebrity, whereas the losers are never mentioned.

If the government used such tactics to tempt alcoholics or smokers, people would be outraged. Rightly so. The government's proper role is to safeguard the people's rights, not to profit from their weakness and gullibility. The fact that the proceeds from gambling are put to good use in no way diminishes the offense of government involvement in it.

State the controlling idea of the article:

_____

_____

_____

_____

_____

_____

_____

Identify relationships among the ideas ("and . . . ," "but . . . ," and so on):

_____

_____

_____

_____

_____

_____

_____

Summarize the article:

_____

_____

_____

_____

_____

_____

_____

A day's pay for a day's work

Every year during football or basketball season, some college in the country makes head-lines when one of its athletes is suspended for violating his amateur status by receiving money. Self-righteous windbags around the country then rant on about the importance of protecting college athletics from professionalism and ensuring that athletes place educa-tion before sports. Not only is that view hypocritical, it's also absurd. The best thing that could happen to college athletics would be for the myth of amateurism to be exposed and the NCAA to abandon its regulation prohibiting pay for play.

To begin with, college athletes have only one reason for going to college—to get a chance to play professional sports. They couldn't care less about an education. Many of them can't read and write, so the courses they take are just warmed-over junior high school subjects. The idea that their education is going to better their position in life is a cruel deception on them. Few others besides athletes are foolish enough to buy such a notion.

Some people argue that if college athletes were paid for playing sports, they would be corrupted. Surely it wouldn't be any less corrupting than the present situation, in which they receive money under the table and in the process violate ethics and the law. And it would spare universities that are supposed to represent society's highest values the embar-rassment and shame that accompany unfavorable newspaper headlines.

The only sensible course of action for the NCAA, and for that matter the Olympic Committee, to take is to discard the phony distinction between amateur and professional. Let colleges run their athletic programs as moneymaking ventures (as many of them now do, dishonestly). Allow them to recruit the best players they can without having to enroll them in academic programs. And permit the players to earn salaries and work full time at their sports. The players will be happier, the teams will perform better, and everyone's consciences will be a lot clearer.

State the controlling idea of the article:

_____

_____

_____

_____

_____

_____

Identify relationships among the ideas ("and . . . ," "but . . . ," and so on):

_____

_____

_____

_____

_____

_____

Summarize the article:

_____

_____

_____

_____

_____

_____

A disservice to everyone

Talk-show TV often displays a mindlessness that's as amazing as it is appalling. One show, for example, featured teenagers who had decided to drop out of high school. The program began with the teens presenting their reasons for quitting, then proceeded to have their parents, a guest expert, and the host try to persuade them to stay in school. Finally, the teens were given a chance to answer the arguments of their elders.

If the show's host and producers thought they were helping solve the problem of high school dropouts, they were mistaken. Appearing on television is an honor few people receive, even if they have made significant contributions to society. Yet those teens received just that honor for threatening to drop out of school. Their foolishness was dignified and they were made to feel like celebrities. Worse, by being allowed to have the last word on the issue, they were given an advantage over the adults.

The chances that those teens changed their minds after the program are slim to none. They very likely had the show videotaped and ran the tape over and over, showing their friends how they held their own in the debate. They may even fantasize that a career in television awaits them. It's not hard to imagine them becoming the heroes of the neighborhood.

Such programs make the jobs of parents and teachers more difficult. Popular culture has already convinced many young people that they know more than their elders, that their opinions have special value, and that learning is a waste of time. Television shows that reinforce such nonsense are surely not a public service. If anything, they are a public disservice.

State the controlling idea of the article:

_____
_____
_____
_____
_____
_____
_____
_____

Identify relationships among the ideas ("and ...," "but ...," and so on):

_____
_____
_____
_____
_____
_____
_____
_____

Summarize the article:

_____
_____
_____
_____
_____
_____
_____

STEP 2: Seek out competing views

Competing views are those that challenge the argument you are evaluating. If you tend to agree with the argument, you will no doubt be tempted to ignore competing views. If you give in to this temptation, you will shortchange the critical thinking process and may deny yourself a valuable insight.

Consider this example. You are examining the argument that slavery was invented by European explorers as a means of dominating Africans and Native Americans. The author supports this claim with hundreds of documented cases. You are so impressed with the case he makes that you are tempted to accept it uncritically.

Resisting this temptation, you look for challenges to this view. You find that a number of sources (for example, Thomas Sowell's *Race and Culture*) claim slavery is thousands of years old, has been practiced on every continent, and is still practiced in the African nations of Ghana, Sudan, and Mauritania. Moreover, these sources maintain that Western culture led the way in *abolishing* slavery.

Whichever view you ultimately decide is more reasonable, you will have benefited by refusing to accept the first argument you encountered.

How to conduct your search

Start by deepening your understanding of the issue. Look up the topic in an encyclopedia devoted to the specific subject. There are encyclopedias of religion and ethics, philosophy, law, medicine, science and technology, and many other topics.

If you can't find a special encyclopedia, consult *Encyclopedia Americana* or *Encyclopaedia Britannica*. Other good general sources are an almanac or *The Monthly Guide to U.S. Publications*.

Next read one or more articles or parts of a few books on the subject.

To find newspaper articles, consult the *New York Times Index*.

To find miscellaneous facts and statistics, consult a good almanac; for example, the *World Almanac*.

To find magazine articles, consult the *Reader's Guide to Periodical Literature*.

To find scholarly articles, consult an index in the specific field, such as the *Social Science Index* or *Humanities Index*.

To find government publications, consult *The Monthly Guide to U.S. Publications*.

To find summaries of articles and books, consult a collection of abstracts, such as *Research in Education* or *Psychological Abstracts*.

Many of these sources and innumerable others are available on the Internet. Here are a few especially helpful websites: **www.askjeeves.com, www.yahoo.com, www.infoplease.com.**

Don't overlook the authorities around you. A number of instructors at your college may have expertise on your topic. If you decide to interview one or more of them, call to make an appointment and state what you want to interview them about and how long you will need.

Here are some tips for conducting the interview.

- Arrive on time and don't overstay your welcome.

- Ask for permission to tape the interview so the instructor will not have to wait while you take notes.

- Avoid asking questions calling for a "yes" or "no" answer. Instead, ask "What do you think about . . . ?" and "What is the basis for your thinking . . . ?"

- Pay attention to the instructor's answers and ask follow-up questions where appropriate.

On the rare occasions when you can't find people with expertise at your college, use your ingenuity. For a medical issue, call the state public health department or the county medical association. The telephone directory will list the numbers of these agencies. Ask to be referred to an appropriate person in your area.

Exercise 27

In Exercise 26 you analyzed essays on gambling, paying college athletes, and TV talk shows. Select one of these essays and seek competing views, using one or more of the research sources listed above. If you agree with the essay, take special care to be thorough in your search. Keep a record of your research. Later exercises will build on this one.

 STEP 3: Sort out disagreements

When you have finished consulting authorities, you may find that they all agree on the issue. In that (very unusual) situation, simply summarize their common view and move on to Step 4.

More often, though, you'll find that authorities disagree on certain aspects of the issue—or on the entire issue. If there are a number of points of disagreement, you'll have to sort them out before you can address them.

The best way to avoid confusion is to make a spreadsheet. Identify the authorities across the top of the page. Then list the aspects of the issue down the left side of the page.

Suppose you're investigating the issue "Should boxing be outlawed?" and you've consulted three individuals in addition to the author of the original argument. The photo on the right shows how your spreadsheet might look.

Note that on the boxing spreadsheet you can tell where the disagreements lie simply by looking across each aspect of the issue. There is no disagreement on the dan-

	MEDICAL DOCTOR	FORMER BOXER	SPORTS JOURNALIST	ORIGINAL ARGUMENT
Is boxing a sport?	No	Yes	Yes	No
Is the intention in boxing to injure the opponent?	Yes	Yes	No	Yes
Is boxing dangerous?	Yes	Yes	Yes	Yes
Can the risk of injury be overcome by training?	No	Yes	Yes	No
Can the risk of injury be overcome by protective gear?	No	No	Yes	No
Would outlawing boxing deny minorities a way out of poverty?	No	Yes	Yes	

ger of boxing, some disagreement on the aspect of intentional harm, and considerable disagreement on the other four aspects.

Wherever your sources disagree, look back at the evidence each offers for that aspect of the issue.

You may be wondering, "Why spend time on each aspect individually when I will eventually have to form an overall view of the issue? Why not deal with the entire issue immediately?"

The answer is that in a complex issue, there can be many insights, and seldom are all of them found on one side. Even a person who is mistaken about the essential aspects of the issue may be right about several lesser aspects. In cases where no single argument is completely sound, you will have to *construct* a better argument than any of the ones you have seen. In order to do this, you will have to be in command of all aspects.

Exercise 28

With the findings you recorded for Exercise 27, make a spreadsheet like the one on boxing shown above. Subsequent exercises will build on this one, so keep a copy of your spreadsheet and your research findings.

STEP 4: Make your judgment

The final step in evaluating an argument is deciding how the original argument compares with competing arguments. Here is how to proceed:

Review the evidence

Begin by reviewing the evidence presented in the original argument, the evidence in competing arguments, and any evidence you discovered yourself. Answer the following questions:

Is all the evidence relevant?   Some items of evidence may be unrelated to the issue. Suppose an aide was asked whether a congresswoman has lied to her constituents. And suppose the aide responds, "Absolutely not," and then proceeds to recite a long list of offenses committed by the person who made the charge.

However interesting the issue of the accuser's behavior may be, it is irrelevant to the issue of whether the congresswoman lied. Whenever you discover evidence that is irrelevant to the issue, disregard it.

Is all the evidence factual?   Errors of fact do not necessarily prove dishonesty. Even well-intentioned, reliable people make mistakes. For example, they may cite out-of-date statistics. Whenever you discover that an item of evidence is unfactual, disregard it.

How comprehensive is the evidence?   When you consult a variety of viewpoints, you usually encounter all important evidence. Still, it is prudent to consider whether any has been overlooked. One good way of doing this is to *consider counterexamples.*

Suppose an author is arguing that parents should not give children responsibilities until they are in their teens, and supports her argument with a number of case histories like this one:

> *I know a person who was given responsibilities such as picking up his clothes and toys at age 3; taking out the garbage at age 6; and raking leaves, washing dishes, and doing laundry at age 10. Today he's in his mid-thirties and he resents having had all those chores.*

A counterexample would be the case of someone (perhaps yourself) who had similar responsibilities in childhood and now regards the experience as valuable. Finding one or more such cases would show that the evidence in the various arguments was not comprehensive.

Is the evidence sufficient to permit a judgment?   To answer this question, look back at the conclusion that the argument is attempting to prove. The more ambitious the claim, the greater the demand for evidence. For example, if the conclusion were, "A relationship *may exist* between disrespect of elders and poor grades in school," a single reputable study would be sufficient evidence.

But suppose the conclusion were expressed more strongly: "A relationship *exists* between disrespect of elders and poor grades in school." This does not assert a possibility but a fact, so more evidence would be required.

If the conclusion were even more sweeping—"Disrespect of elders *causes* young people to have poor grades in school"—the demand for evidence would be even greater.

Test the conclusion for reasonableness

Chapter One presented several ways to test ideas for reasonableness. (The term used for the ideas discussed there, "opinion," has the same essential meaning as "judgment" or "conclusion.") Two of those ways are especially relevant here:

1. *Think of situations to which the conclusion ought to apply and decide whether it does apply.* When testing the opinion that truth is relative, we considered a variety of situations. Among them were Galileo's conclusion that the earth revolves around the sun, the existence of concentration camps, and the authenticity of the painting entitled, *The Man with the Golden Helmet.*

2. *Think of exceptions to the claim set forth in the conclusion.* To test the conclusion, "You are the only thing that is real. Everything else is your imagination," we considered some things that are outside ourselves yet nevertheless very real.

Now we'll consider additional ways to test a conclusion:

Reverse the conclusion.   That is, take the exact opposite of the conclusion and try to make a case for it.

Let's say the conclusion you are testing is, "People must feel good about themselves before they can achieve in school or in life." [You may recognize this as a tenet of the self-esteem movement.]   ·

The reverse of this conclusion is, "People must achieve in school or in life before they can feel good about themselves." Your case for this might include examples of how achievement builds confidence, even at an early age. Relevant examples would be a child learning to eat with a spoon, walk, tie shoelaces, ride a bike, and read.

Consider the implications.   Think about related ideas suggested by the conclusion. (Finding negative ones will help you see flaws you might otherwise miss.)

Let's say the conclusion is, "What people view in movies or on television has no effect on their behavior." (Media spokespeople often say this in response to complaints that graphic sex and violence have a negative social impact.)

The implications of this conclusion are that viewing films and television programs can neither degrade nor inspire or motivate us. But if that were really the case, then public service announcements to drive sober and practice safe sex would be pointless and advertisers would be wasting millions of dollars on them.

Consider the consequences.   That is, think of what would be likely to happen if the conclusion were put into practice.

Suppose the conclusion you are examining is, "The welfare system that continues to drain our tax dollars should not be gradually phased out but ended immediately."

Here are some of the likely consequences: (1) some able-bodied welfare recipients would seek work and find it; (2) others would be less successful in their search; (3) those who are too old or too ill to work would be left with no source of income; (4) the living conditions for some children on welfare would decline; (5) private agencies such as the Salvation Army would increase their giving, but this might not meet the need.

Not all of these tests fit every type of conclusion. You must decide which are appropriate in specific instances.

Shape your judgment to fit your analysis

When your analysis demonstrates that the original argument or one of the competing arguments is completely sound and therefore needs no revision, you can simply state that fact and explain how your analysis confirmed it.

If, however, you find that *none* of the arguments is entirely sound, your challenge will be to combine insights from the various views.

After combining the insights of the individuals you consulted on the boxing issue, your final assessment might be this:

> *Boxing is not properly classified as a sport because the contestants intend to injure each other. Thus, boxing is more dangerous than sport, in which injuries occur accidentally or because rules are broken. It's true that training and protective gear can reduce the threat to fighters but not eliminate it. For these reasons, I believe boxing should be outlawed. I admit that such action would deny members of minority groups one way of rising above poverty, but better ways can and should be created.*

Let's look at a new issue for another example of how to construct a new argument that combines insights.

The argument you are analyzing is, "Women's athletic teams at Progress University should not receive an equal share of the sports budget because men's teams play a more competitive schedule and draw larger crowds at athletic events."

The main opposing argument, you find, is, "Women's athletic teams at Progress University *should* receive an equal share of the sports budget because the present budget is discriminatory."

Among the significant facts your analysis uncovered are these:

1. In past years, the budget was determined first and the teams' schedules were set accordingly. Women were forced to play less competitive schedules simply because their travel allowance was modest.

2. The attendance at women's athletic events has tripled over the past five years. It is now 65% of men's teams' attendance, despite the "softer" schedule.

3. The courts have consistently ruled in favor of more equitable treatment of women athletes.

4. If the budget were divided equally next year, the men's program could not be maintained at its present level.

Shaping your judgment to fit your findings, you produce a new argument, one that reflects the valid points made by each of the opposing sides. Your argument is as follows:

*Women's teams at Progress University should receive an increasing share
of the athletic budget each year for the next three years. After three years
their share should be equal to that received by the men's teams. By gradually increasing the women's share of the budget, the school can maintain
the men's athletic program at its present level while the budget is worked
out. Additional sources of support should be sought so that, if possible, the
desired end of equity can be achieved sooner.*

In both the boxing and the women's athletics example, of course, your arguments would be expanded beyond the summaries shown here.

In all your evaluative work, it is vital that you accept the limitations of analysis. Only rarely can you be certain that one view of an issue is correct. More often,
the best you can achieve is probability. That is, you can show only that one view is
more reasonable than the others. In some cases, all you will have is a number of
possibilities, all supported by the evidence, but no one more so than the others. In
these situations, prudence demands that you withhold judgment until more evidence
is available.

Exercise 29

In Exercise 26 you examined essays on gambling, paying college athletes, and TV talk shows. In Exercises 27 and 28 you continued your
analysis of one of those essays. Now you are ready to complete your
analysis by making your judgment, as shown in this section. Write your
response on a separate sheet of paper.

Exercise 30

Read the three arguments that follow. Then choose one argument and
apply the four-step approach explained in this chapter. Record the results of your testing in the space provided. Then, on a separate sheet of
paper, write a composition of at least three paragraphs discussing the
strengths and weaknesses of the original passage. Present what you
find to be the most reasonable view of the issue. (You may wish to
consult Chapter Seven, "Expressing Ideas Persuasively.")

Argument 1:
*It's no wonder that crime is out of control in this society and honest citizens live in fear. The
prison system is no longer a deterrent to crime. In some cases it almost encourages crime.
Inmates are given excellent food and comfortable cells furnished with cable television.
Their medical and dental needs are provided for without cost. Prisoners can use library and
exercise facilities.*

*Often inmates do no hard labor in exchange for these benefits. They're free to relax and
enjoy themselves while taxpayers toil to pay the bill.*

The situation is not only absurd but intolerable. Since the rehabilitation approach doesn't work, prisons should punish criminals. And the first step is to end the country club atmosphere. Remove all the comforts. If we make the prison experience miserable, people will think not once but several times before committing a crime.

Argument 2:
Should editors of college newspapers be allowed to make all their own decisions? Some people say yes. By making decisions, they reason, editors learn a sense of responsibility. This argument overlooks the harm a careless decision can do.

If an editor decides to publish a story with a racist message, every minority student on campus will be insulted and outraged. If the editor publishes a defense of male chauvinism, every woman on campus will feel wronged. If the editor publishes a story that mocks religion, every religious student will be offended. In all three cases, the newspaper encourages the very intolerance that education is supposed to conquer.

Editors of college newspapers are not professional journalists. They're merely students learning another subject, in this case journalism. Therefore, they should not be allowed to make important editorial decisions. Such decisions should be made by faculty advisors.

Argument 3:
Recently the faculty of a school district in a northeastern state voted unanimously to reject merit pay awards. The faculty did not object to the amount of the awards. They objected to the very idea of determining who the best teachers are and giving them, in effect, a bonus for excellence.

The faculty in that school district acted wisely and courageously. It does not matter how the selection is made; selecting some faculty for merit awards implies that others are not as deserving. That implication hurts feelings, creates dissension, and undermines faculty morale. In the long run it results in poorer education for students.

Whenever a school board has money to give faculty, it should be divided among all teachers. That would convey an encouraging message to teachers: "You're all doing an excellent job."

Your testing:

_____

_____

_____

_____

_____

_____

_____

_____

_____

_____

_____

_____

_____

Exercise 31

Read the arguments that follow. Then choose one argument and apply the four-step approach explained in this chapter. Record the results of your testing in the space provided. Then, on a separate sheet of paper, write a composition of at least three paragraphs discussing the strengths and weaknesses of the original passage. Present what you find to be the most reasonable view of the issue. (You may wish to consult Chapter Seven, "Expressing Ideas Persuasively.")

Argument 1:
The headline screams "Binge Drinking Soars Among College Women." Increasing numbers of college women, it seems, purposely drink to get drunk. And being drunk makes them more vulnerable to casual sex, pregnancy, and sexually transmitted diseases including AIDS, not to mention rape. The amazing thing is not the report itself but the response of many journalists and social analysts, who wring their collective hands, scratch their collective heads, and ask why, what can possibly explain this development?

The answer may elude these professionals, but it's clear enough to many less sophisticated Americans. Youthful binge drinkers are simply following the advice they've received from the media all their lives. Reebok counsels them, "Life is short—play hard." Nike sells them T-shirts that advise "Just do it." Psychologists tell them, "Whatever feels good is good; follow your feelings." Anyone who is surprised that ideas have consequences needs a remedial course in reality.

Argument 2:
TV and movie apologists are forever telling us that we have no business criticizing them because they are only holding a mirror up to reality. Many people buy that explanation, but they shouldn't. It would be more accurate to say the media hold a magnifying glass to carefully selected realities—namely, the most outrageous and sensational events of the day, such as O. J. Simpson's trial, Princess Diana's tragic death, and President Clinton's sexual activities and alleged obstruction of justice among them.

Consider how this happens. The first platoon of media people report the latest sensational story as it unfolds, squeezing each new development for all the airtime or newsprint it will yield. Meanwhile, agents and attorneys are negotiating the sale of movie and TV rights to the story. The sleazier the story, the greater the payoff. After the movie is produced, every situation comedy, detective show, and western drama builds an episode around the successful theme. So a single despicable, disgusting act—real or imagined—can generate months of sensational media fare.

In short, the media exploit our social problems for ratings, feed us a steady diet of debasing material, celebrate irresponsible behavior, and then have the audacity to blame parents and teachers for the social problems that result.

Argument 3:
Many employers limit access to the Internet by controlling which employees can use it, as well as what content they can read. These employers argue that the Internet is a serious

business tool that only some people understand well enough to use effectively. Others, they contend, use the Internet only to waste time and avoid work.

Employees who want to waste time, however, will find a way to do so. All employees need access to the Internet so they can keep up on current and company events, assess the competition, and use other business-related tools. The employees themselves are the best ones to manage their time and resources, determining what is and is not useful in getting their work done.

Your testing:

_____

_____

_____

_____

_____

_____

_____

_____

_____

_____

_____

_____

_____

Practicing Critical Thinking 9

In Practicing Critical Thinking 8 in Chapter Two you listed a number of observations to be examined more closely later. Look back at that list, select one of those observations, and restate it on a separate sheet of paper. Then follow the appropriate guide to reflection:

a) If you chose an *issue*, identify the various views people take on it and the evidence they offer in support of those views. Look for additional evidence and decide which view of the issue is most reasonable.

b) If you chose a *statement that seemed insightful*, think of appropriate ways to test the statement. Carry out the test(s) and decide whether the statement really is insightful.

c) If you chose a *statement that you suspected was shallow or mistaken* because it was at odds with your experience, think of ways to test the statement. Then carry out the test(s) and decide whether the statement really is insightful.

d) If you chose a *matter that you wished to understand more fully*, do the necessary research and record what you learn.

Practicing Critical Thinking 10

By now your observations are probably becoming both more frequent and more numerous. On a separate sheet of paper list your most recent observations in each of the following categories. (Save this list for a later assignment.)

a) Interesting issues you would like to address when you have more time

b) Statements that appear to be unusually insightful (they may have been made by authors, instructors, fellow students, or someone else)

c) Statements that seem shallow or mistaken

d) Anything you have experienced or heard about that you wish to understand more fully such as an incident, a process, or a procedure

Name _____ Date _____ / _____ / _____

1   Would it be accurate to define an argument as a dispute characterized by angry exchanges? Explain.

2   Not all writing presents arguments. True or False? Explain.

3   When is an argument persuasive to critical thinkers?

4   According to this chapter, the first step in evaluating a longer argument is understanding the argument. What are the other three steps?

5   Explain the approach this chapter presents for understanding an argument.

6   What are features of an effective summary?

7 What are open-ended questions, and when does this chapter suggest you use them?

8 What is the most important resource available in any library?

9 When you consult authorities and find that they disagree about an issue, you may become confused. What tip does this chapter offer for overcoming such confusion?

10 When the evidence offered in support of an opinion is inadequate, you can be certain the opinion is mistaken. True or False? Explain.

11 This chapter added several new ways to test opinions for reasonableness to those presented in Chapter One. What are the new ways?

Answers to this quiz may be found at http://college.hmco.com.

4

Solving Problems

Cultivate creativity

The scene is a Nazi concentration camp during World War II. A young boy is directed to the left, the death line. He follows the other prisoners into the special barracks that will house them until execution. There is only one door and that is guarded by armed soldiers. How can he possibly escape certain death?

Looking around the barracks, he spots a pail of water and a brush. He gets them, falls to his knees, and begins scrubbing the floor, slowly backing closer to the door. Then, still scrubbing, he backs his way out the door and down the steps.

At the bottom the boy stands and slowly walks away, pail in hand. Once across the yard, he mingles with a group of other prisoners. Though the guards have seen his every move, rather than question him they assume he was assigned to scrub the barracks.

This true story is recounted by the man it happened to, Samuel Pisar, in his book *Blood of Hope.* It is a dramatic example of creative problem solving.

For ages creativity was considered the special talent of a small number of fortunate individuals. If you have been led to believe that you are one of the unfortunate ones, you've probably never tried to be creative. That's reasonable. Why strive for the impossible?

The good news is that old notion about creativity was wrong! Modern scholarship has shown that creativity is largely a skill that *anyone can learn.* And you don't need a high IQ to learn it.

While we're at it, let's correct some other common misconceptions:

The misconception that creativity applies only to the arts. The fact is creativity has application to any activity from gardening and cooking to parenting, scientific research, and inventing products and services.

The misconception that alcohol and drugs help creativity. In reality, they cloud the mind and suppress creativity.

The misconception that you have to be a little loony to be creative. Most authorities agree that creativity demonstrates mental health rather than illness.

Now let's explore how you can develop your creativity and solve problems in school, at work, and in your personal life.

See problems as opportunities

Problems have a way of occurring at inopportune times and interrupting the flow of our lives. Not surprisingly, our first reaction to them is usually a feeling of frustration and annoyance.

Many people get trapped in that reaction. They never get far beyond complaining about things that don't work properly; people who have offended them; personal needs that aren't being met; difficulties in school, at work, in the community, in the nation, and in the world.

Ironically, this response does nothing to improve the situation. It only succeeds in making them feel miserable.

Effective problem solvers react differently. When they realize things aren't going the way they expect or want, they don't waste time lamenting their misfortune. Instead, they look for solutions.

During the California Gold Rush of the 1850s, Levi Strauss brought a supply of heavyweight canvas to the bustling gold fields, hoping to sell it to miners for tents. When the miners weren't interested, he didn't brood—he created the durable trousers we know as Levi jeans.

Many other inventions arose out of similar problem situations.

Arthur Scott invented the paper towel when his company received a shipment of paper that was too heavy and wrinkled to be used for its bathroom tissue.

George Safford Parker designed a dependable fountain pen after being disappointed with the leaky pens of his day.

Dr. Henry Heimlich devised the life-saving maneuver that bears his name after witnessing the ineffectiveness of existing responses to choking on food.

Francis McNamara invented the credit card after suffering the embarrassment of taking clients to dinner and realizing he didn't have enough money with him to pay the bill.

Edwin Land invented the Polaroid Land camera because his daughter didn't like waiting for pictures to be developed.

What do all these examples have in common? The obvious answer is *ingenuity*. All the people involved used their imagination to produce a creative solution.

But these examples have one more thing in common, something that provided the motivation to think creatively. That something is *dissatisfaction*. People don't invest time and effort changing things that are working well or improving what doesn't need improvement. *Before they will bother, they have to be bothered!*

To be an effective problem solver, you will have to view frustrations, annoyances, and aggravations positively. Think of them as encouragements to creativity, spurs to achievement. The following exercises will help you adopt this perspective.

Exercise 32

List all the frustrations, annoyances, and aggravations you have experienced lately.

_____
_____
_____
_____
_____

Exercise 33

Now list all the complaints you have heard others make about people and things, including processes and procedures.

_____
_____
_____
_____
_____
_____
_____
_____

Nurture your curiosity

In 1935, Paul Sperry took his cocker spaniel for a walk. The ground was covered with snow and ice, and Sperry had difficulty keeping his footing. But he noticed that the dog had no such difficulty.

Inquisitive, Sperry examined the pattern on the bottom of the dog's paws. Later he carved that pattern into a piece of crepe rubber and created the sole of what is today known as the boat shoe.

Similarly, in 1948, after a walk in the woods, Swiss engineer George de Mestral found that cockleburs had stuck to his socks. Surely millions of people had that same experience and merely cursed their misfortune. But de Mestral wondered what made them stick, so he put them under a microscope and saw hundreds of tiny hooks that grasped anything with loops, such as cloth.

Putting that insight to work, de Mestral invented a method of duplicating nature's hooks and loops. The resulting product is known today as Velcro.

What Sperry, de Mestral, and other creative people have in common is curiosity, the desire for knowledge. What sets curious people apart from others is the habit of asking questions.

As a small child, you were no doubt filled with questions—"What is that, Mommy? Why is it that way? Who made it so? Why not some other way?" and so on.

If you are like most people, you stopped being inquisitive quite early. Perhaps your parents discouraged your questions. Or your teachers may have given you so much information to remember that you saw no need to seek more. In any case, you can regain your curiosity.

The following questions are especially useful in stimulating curiosity, and they are applicable to a wide variety of situations:

1. **What caused this to happen?**

This question is often associated with assigning blame, but it has a much more positive use than that. Scientists use it to probe the mysteries of the universe; social scientists, to interpret human behavior; doctors, to form diagnoses; historians, to make sense of human events. The same question will help you to better understand the problems that confront you. The relationship between causes and effects can be very complex, of course, so be wary of convenient, oversimplified answers.

2. **What stages occurred in the development of this?**

Most things have a long and interesting history. Consider, for example, writing instruments. The first such device was probably a rock used to put a marking on a cave wall. (The exact inscription may have been "Ug loves Ula," but we can't be sure.) From that crude instrument, many devices have resulted. The stylus, quill pen, fountain pen, ball point pen, pencil, felt tip pen, typewriter, personal computer, laptop computer, and Palm Pilot.

The more you consider the history of the things around you, the more you will appreciate the miracle of human inventiveness.

3. **What improvements might be made in this?**

What kinds of inventions do people get patents for? If you're thinking "new products," you're only partly right. Patents are also issued for *improvements on existing products*. In fact, the great majority of the patents issued by the U.S. Patent Office are for improvements.

Nothing that humans have ever invented is perfect. This applies not only to products such as cars, computers, and telephones. It also applies to procedures, processes, and even concepts such as taxation, progress, and liberty.

Believe it or not, human imperfection has a positive side. It guarantees that the opportunities for creative achievement are neverending.

Exercise 34

List some important events about which you might ask, "What caused this to happen?" If you have difficulty thinking of any, consider recent news stories you've read or seen.

_____

_____

_____

_____

_____

_____

_____

_____

_____

Exercise 35

List some things that make your life easier. For example, your coffee maker, your electric razor, and your car.

_____

_____

_____

_____

_____

_____

_____
_____
_____
_____
_____

Exercise 36

Select one item from your list in Exercise 35. Then, identify as many of
the earlier stages in its evolution as you can, as shown in the example
of writing instruments. (Tip: Start with the item you listed and ask
what preceded it, then what preceded that, and so on as far back in
time as you can go.)

_____
_____
_____
_____
_____
_____
_____
_____

Exercise 37

List some procedures and processes you are familiar with. For example,
the procedure for getting a driver's license or earning a college degree.

_____
_____
_____
_____
_____
_____
_____
_____

Exercise 38

Select one of the things you listed in Exercise 35 or the procedures or processes you listed in Exercise 37. Then list some improvements that might be made.

_____

_____

_____

_____

_____

_____

_____

_____

_____

_____

A problem-solving strategy

Here is a simple, effective strategy that combines creativity and critical thinking. It is a proven method of problem solving:

Step 1: Look for problems

Do you know what a *crisis* is? A little problem that was allowed to grow and grow until it became too big to ignore. Little problems are much easier and less costly to solve than big ones, so it makes sense to identify them early. Doing so is not difficult. Just challenge yourself to find them. Don't limit your search to problems that affect you personally. Look, too, for problems that affect other individuals and people in general.

Tomorrow morning when you get up, say to yourself, "In the past I haven't paid much attention to problems. Today I'm going to notice as many as I can."

Whenever you feel frustration, annoyance, or disappointment, or you hear others express those feelings, scribble a brief note for later reference. A few key words should be enough to help you recall the problem later. For example, if you keep having difficulty finding a parking place on campus, you might write "parking: ... argh!" If you serve on a committee with a pushy person, just write "dealing with Laura."

Later, when you can spare the time, review your list of problems, select one, and proceed with the next step.

Step 2: Express the problem

"A problem well stated," observed Henry Hazlitt, "is half solved." He realized that each expression of a problem creates its own path toward solution. No two paths are exactly alike.

The problem of drunken driving, for example, might be expressed in any of the following ways, among others:

1. How can we most effectively punish drunken drivers?

2. How can we educate people about the effects of drunken driving?

3. How can we persuade people to take the car keys away from friends who have had too much to drink?

4. How can we convince people that alcohol seriously affects their reflexes?

5. How can we make cars impossible for a drunken person to operate?

Notice that question 1 leads to ideas for punishment; question 2, to educational ideas; questions 3 and 4, to explanations or persuasive strategies; question 5, to modifications in cars rather than drivers.

Which is the best expression? We can't say until after we have produced many ideas for each expression and evaluated all the ideas.

This much, however, is clear—the question that focuses on punishment is not likely to produce ideas for education or for modifying cars. The key to getting a variety of different and unusual ideas is to ask a number of different *questions.*

Notice, too, that although questions 1–5 differ in their focus, their form is the same: Each question asks, "How can . . . ?" That is the best way to express a problem because it focuses on action. Other questions, such as "Why?" and "What?," are useful in other ways, but inappropriate for expressing problems. The reason is that they focus on understanding instead of action.

Step 3: Investigate, as necessary

The first source of information to consult in problem solving is yourself. Even if you have little or no specific knowledge about the problem confronting you, you may have related knowledge. Given all your personal experiences and observations (plus all you have learned from other people, read about, or seen on television), chances are you have a wealth of insight to draw upon. Some of it may apply to the problem at hand.

The trick, of course, is to *identify* your relevant insights. This can be difficult if, like most people, you classify your knowledge narrowly.

Try to break down artificial barriers between areas of knowledge. Form the habit of asking yourself, "What have I learned in other situations that might be helpful in this one?"

After reviewing your own experience, consult people who have special knowledge of the subject. If your first reaction is, "I don't know such people," think again. Every faculty member of your college has significant expertise in his or her subject. Your friends and acquaintances likely have special qualifications in one field or another—law, medicine, accounting, landscaping, carpentry, and so on.

For other sources of knowledge, see the suggestions listed in the section "Seek out competing views" (Chapter Three). Or consult your campus librarian.

Whatever you need to know, there are people who can inform you, and they are often much closer than you might imagine.

Step 4: List possible solutions

The first solutions that come to mind are usually the most familiar and common ones, the ones that have been tried and found to be unsatisfactory. To be creative you must get beyond these. As Linus Pauling expressed it, "The best way to have a good idea is to have lots of ideas." Here's how to get lots of ideas:

1. After listing the common, familiar solutions, list as many new and different possibilities as you can, ones you've never heard before.

2. Read your list of solutions aloud and think of as many additional associations as you can.

3. Examine the problem again and ask what it reminds you of. Where appropriate, also ask what it looks, sounds, or functions like. These questions will often produce analogies that stimulate idea-production.

4. Consider combining two or more possible solutions in an unusual way.

5. Try to visualize what the situation would be like if the problem were overcome and study that image for clues to the solution.

While you are taking these steps, resist the temptation to analyze each idea as it comes to you. Doing so interrupts the flow of ideas and may result in your rejecting a creative idea simply because it is unfamiliar. Postpone all evaluation until you have completed your list of possible solutions.

Don't settle for a modest number of ideas—doing so is the most common characteristic of *uncreative* thinking. Remember that the more ideas you produce, the better your chance of producing a really good one.

Step 5: Refine your best solution

Review your list and choose the solutions that seem most promising. For each of these ideas, answer the following questions:

When, where, and by whom would it be carried out?

How would it be accomplished, step by step?

How would it be financed?

What additional people, materials, and equipment, if any, would be required?

What changes would this solution necessitate?

The answers to these questions will help you decide which solution is most effective and practical.

Once you have decided on a solution, look for imperfections in it and consider the complications that could arise in implementing it.

If you have difficulty being objective about your own ideas, adopt the view of people who would object to your idea. Challenge your idea as they would by asking questions like these:

Will this solution solve the entire problem or only part of it?

Will the solution be permanent or only temporary?

Is the cost of implementation prohibitive?

Will the solution disrupt other functions or cause dissension?

Will the solution compromise safety?

After answering these questions, decide what modifications of your solution would overcome all reasonable objections. If such objections cannot be overcome, you may have to consider a different solution.

The diagram on page 100 illustrates a format that will help you apply the problem-solving strategy presented in this section to any problem. Since Step 1 is your ongoing search for problems, this diagram begins with Step 2.

Expression of the problem

How can _____

How can _____

How can _____

How can _____

How can _____

Key facts from your investigation

_____

_____

_____

_____

_____

_____

Possible solutions

_____

_____

_____

_____

_____

_____

_____

_____

_____

_____

_____

Refinement of your best solution

_____

_____

_____

_____

_____

_____

_____

_____

_____

Exercise 39

On a separate sheet of paper, solve this problem using the problem-solving format illustrated on page 100.

Changes are often made in the rules and procedures of sports. Choose your favorite sport and imagine you are a member of the rules committee considering how to make the sport more challenging or exciting to play, as well as more enjoyable to watch.

Exercise 40

On a separate sheet of paper, solve this problem using the problem-solving format illustrated on page 100.

You work for a toy company and are asked by your supervisor to design a new toy. She gives you these instructions: "When you submit your proposal, explain what existing toy it most closely resembles and how it differs from that toy. (The more differences it has, the more original it will be.) Include a sketch of the new toy, state its name, and identify the age group it will appeal to."

Exercise 41

On a separate sheet of paper, solve this problem using the problem-solving format illustrated on page 100.

Even though effective listening is an important skill in school and in careers, studies show that the average person listens with between 25% and 50% accuracy. You are a parent who would like to ensure that your infant will develop good listening skills as she grows. Solve this problem as you did earlier exercises in this chapter.

Exercise 42

On a separate sheet of paper, solve this problem using the problem-solving format illustrated on page 100.

Your challenge is to create a new game. It may be a parlor game such as checkers or Monopoly, a table game like ping pong or pool, or a field game like soccer or baseball. Use the problem–solving approach you used in earlier exercises in this chapter. Be sure to explain the rules, procedures, and purpose of your game clearly. If it requires a special playing board, court, or field, include a diagram.

Exercise 43

List all the things you use daily, including even small things such as the toothpaste tube and the vegetable peeler. Make an asterisk by each item that has caused you frustration or dissatisfaction because of its design. Then select one of the items you marked and treat it as a problem to be solved. Solve the problem on a separate sheet of paper, using the format illustrated on page 100.

Exercise 44

Two main causes of divorce are carelessness in selecting a marriage partner and ignorance of the demands of marriage and parenthood. In many cases, the home, the school, and the church are not meeting the challenge of preparing young people for marriage. Treat this as a problem and solve it on a separate sheet of paper, using the format illustrated on page 100.

Exercise 45

From time to time the larger fast-food chains—McDonald's, Burger King, Wendy's, among others—introduce a new food item. Examples include the Big Mac, the Egg McMuffin, the Whopper, and Chicken Mc-Nuggets. Imagine that you work for one of these chains and have been challenged to create a new food item, give it an appealing name, and design an advertising campaign for it. Use a separate sheet of paper and follow the format illustrated on page 100.

Exercise 46

You live in a small mountain town, population 1,400, situated more than 150 miles from the nearest city. For more than a year the town has been without a physician. You are heading a committee responsible for finding a doctor who would be willing to locate there. Use a separate sheet of paper and follow the format illustrated on page 100.

Exercise 47

This country has a growing population of retired people whose life experience and professional expertise are unique resources. Unfortunately, those resources are virtually untapped. When people retire, society assumes they can no longer be productive and ignores their talents. Ironically, many retired people are not only able but also willing and even eager to make a contribution. Solve this problem on a separate sheet of paper, using the format illustrated on page 100.

Exercise 48

Identify a current unsolved problem in your major field of study. Solve the problem on a separate sheet of paper, following the format illustrated on page 100.

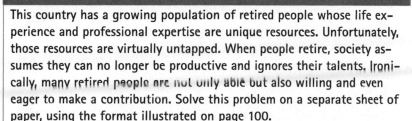

Practicing Critical Thinking 11

Someone once said that the simple prescription for success is to find a need that is not being met and find a way to meet it. The examples noted in the chapter show that the prescription works. Your challenge in this critical thinking practice is to apply the prescription. Consider the unmet needs on your campus, in your community, in a workplace you are familiar with, in the nation and world. (Tip: People's complaints often point to such needs.) Be sure to think broadly, considering the need for products, services, procedures, and systems. List your findings.

Quiz

1 Creativity applies only to the arts. True or False? Explain.

2 Explain the relationship between dissatisfaction and creativity.

3 List three questions that are especially helpful in stimulating creativity.

4 State and briefly explain each of the steps this chapter recommends for problem solving.

Step One:

Step Two:

Quiz (continued)

Step Three:

Step Four:

Step Five:

Answers to this quiz may be found at http://college.hmco.com.

In this chapter

Three kinds of errors

Be alert for errors of perception, judgment, and reaction.

Errors of perception

Errors often begin in faulty ways of seeing the world—"mine is better" thinking, selective perception, gullibility and skepticism, bias, pretending to know, and either/or thinking.

Errors of judgment

Double standard, irrelevant criterion, overgeneralizing or stereotyping, hasty conclusion, unwarranted assumption, failure to make a distinction, and oversimplification are the main kinds of judgment errors.

Errors of reaction

When we explain away ideas, shift the burden of proof, attack the person, or set up a "straw man," we risk fooling ourselves.

Errors can multiply

Any error in thinking invites additional errors.

5

Recognizing Errors in Thinking

3 kinds of errors

Most often people seek in life occasions for persisting in their opinions
rather than for educating themselves. Each of us looks for justification in
the event. The rest, which runs counter to that opinion, is overlooked. . . .
It seems as if the mind enjoys nothing more than sinking deeper into error.

André Gide

Perhaps Gide overstated the problem in suggesting that we *enjoy* error. But he was wise in noting our difficulty in dealing with issues objectively and logically. To overcome that difficulty, we need to understand the kinds of errors that can entrap us and the steps we can take to avoid them.

Three broad types of errors are common: errors of perception, errors of judgment, and errors of reaction.

Errors of perception

Errors of perception are not blunders made while examining issues. They are faulty ways of seeing reality, preventing us from being open-minded even before we begin to apply our critical thinking. The following are especially serious.

"Mine is better" thinking

As small children we may have said "My mommy is prettier than any other mommy" or "My daddy is bigger and stronger." Perhaps we had similar thoughts about our houses, toys, and finger paintings.

Now that we've gotten older, we probably don't express "mine is better" thinking. Yet we may still indulge in it. Such thinking often occurs in matters that are important to us, such as our race, religion, ethnic group, social class, political party, or philosophy of life.

This habit is not always obvious. In fact, "mine is better" thinking can be quite subtle. We may be quite uninterested in a person until we find out she is Irish, like us. Suddenly we feel a sense of kinship. We may think a person is rather dense until he says something that matches our view. Then we decide he's really quite bright after all.

"Mine is better" thinking is natural and often harmless. Even so, this kind of thinking creates distance between people through a win-lose mentality, which can easily prevent you from learning from others. To prevent this, remember that opening your mind to ideas from other people can broaden your perspective and lead to fresh insights. Give every idea a fair hearing—even an idea that challenges your own.

Selective perception

In one sense, we see selectively most of the time. Let's say you and two friends, a horticulture major and an art major, walk through a shopping mall. You want to buy a pair of shoes; the others are just taking a break from studying. The same reality exists for each of you: stores, potted plants, people passing by. Still, each of you focuses on different things. While you are looking for shoe stores, one friend notices plants. The other studies faces for interesting features.

Later, one of you says, "Hey, did you see the big new store in the mall?" The others say no. Though the store was before all of your eyes, two of you screened it out.

That kind of selective perception is often harmless. Another kind of selective perception takes place when we focus on things that support our current ideas and reject anything that challenges them. Suppose someone thinks that a particular ethnic group is stupid, violent, cheap, or lazy. Then "stupid" behaviors will capture that person's attention. And if his bias is strong enough, he will completely miss intelligent behaviors from members of that group. He'll see only evidence that supports his prejudice.

You can break the habit of selective perception by looking and listening for details you haven't seen before. Also press yourself to balance your perception. If you find yourself focusing on negative details, look for positive ones, and vice versa.

Gullibility and skepticism

Philosopher Alfred Korzybski observed, "there are two ways to slide easily through life: to believe everything or to doubt everything—both ways save us from thinking." To believe everything we are told is to be gullible. To doubt everything is to be skeptical.

An alternative to gullibility and skepticism is questioning. This means greeting all ideas with curiosity and wonder, judging none of them in advance, and being equally prepared to find wisdom, foolishness, or some combination of the two.

Bias toward the majority or the minority

Bias tends to follow our affections. If we feel more comfortable with the majority on our side, we may choose the majority view. If we identify with the underdog and love the challenge of confronting superior numbers, we may embrace the minority view.

Each of these choices can occur with little or no awareness of our underlying bias. And in each case we put feelings of comfort and personal preference above the evidence. Critical thinking means deciding issues on their merits rather than on the number or the celebrity status of the people on the opposing sides.

Pretending to know

Some people believe that confessing ignorance makes them look ineffective, so they pretend to know things they really don't. After a while, pretending becomes a habit that hinders critical thinking. Suppose someone says on several occasions, "I've read quite a few books on psychology." Also suppose the truth is different and he's never read a book on the subject. The idea will become so familiar that he might take it for the truth. What's more, he'll begin to confuse his guesses about psychology with real knowledge. Practice staying aware of your statements and remaining alert for pretense. Whenever you find it, acknowledge the truth and resolve not to lie to yourself or others again.

Bias for or against change

According to an old joke, conservatives have never met a new idea they liked, and liberals have never met a new idea they didn't like. Each observation contains an element of truth.

Some people find even small changes, like returning home from school and finding the furniture rearranged, very upsetting. Major changes, like moving across the country, can be even more disturbing.

New ideas can have a similar effect on such people. Old beliefs provide a sense of comfort and security. When those beliefs are challenged, people may feel that reality has been pulled out from under them. That's probably why ancient rulers killed the bearers of bad news. It's also one reason why persuading others can be difficult.

Bias against change may be older and more common than bias for change. Yet the latter seems to be increasing today, perhaps because technology is advancing so rapidly. Some people think that old ideas, old beliefs, old values are of little use today. For them, new is always better.

Neither perspective is consistent with critical thinking. Some new ideas are clearly better than the old ones they replace. Progress has in fact occurred in every area of life, including science, technology, education, and government. Yet this reality has another, less fortunate side. New ideas sometimes contain serious flaws that go unnoticed at first. Time and experience sometimes prove that the supposed great leap forward was actually several steps backward.

To avoid bias for or against change, know your own mental habits. Also resist the temptation to accept first impressions.

Either/or thinking

This error of perception means taking only extreme positions on an issue when other positions are possible. For example, one person thinks that accepting evolution means rejecting the idea of creation. Another person thinks that being Republican means taking a conservative stance on every issue.

Yet it's possible to believe in evolution and creation. You could believe that God created the universe and planned for it to evolve over millions of years. (You could also be a Republican without always taking a conservative stand.)

Either/or thinking hampers critical thinking. This error forces us to take extreme, unreasonable views. To avoid either/or thinking, look for times when there seem to be only two possible views. Ask yourself, "Are these the only possibilities? Could another view be more reasonable—perhaps one that includes elements of both?"

An example is the debate over crime prevention. Some elected officials argue for banning assault weapons and registering handguns. The National Rifle Association argues for getting criminals off the street. You might ask, "Why not take both actions and add others, such as building more prisons, as well?"

Exercise 49

Consider each of the seven errors of perception. Think of a time when you've committed each one and describe these situations. Explain how you reacted and what consequences followed. Then decide how you might have avoided the error and how the consequences could have been different.

Chapter 5

"Mine is better" thinking

_____

_____

_____

_____

_____

_____

Selective perception

_____

_____

_____

_____

_____

_____

Gullibility and skepticism

_____

_____

_____

_____

_____

Bias toward the majority or the minority

_____

_____

_____

_____

_____

Bias for or against change

_____
_____
_____
_____
_____
_____

Pretending to know

_____
_____
_____
_____
_____

Either/or thinking

_____
_____
_____
_____
_____
_____

Errors of judgment

Errors of judgment occur in the process of sorting out and assessing evidence. They prevent us from reaching the most reasonable conclusion. The following errors of judgment are among the most common.

Double standard

This error consists of using one standard of judgment for our ideas and an entirely different, more demanding standard for ideas that conflict with ours.

People who employ a double standard ignore inconsistencies, contradictions, and outrageous overstatements in arguments they agree with. Yet they nitpick their opponents' arguments. They even use different vocabularies. Allies are described as "imaginative," "forceful," and "brutally honest." Opponents with the same qualities are labeled "utopian," "belligerent," or "mean-spirited."

Critical thinking demands a single standard of judgment for both those who agree and those who disagree with us.

Irrelevant criterion

This error consists of criticizing an idea because it fails to do what it wasn't intended to do. Say that a chief executive proposes a new reward program for employees' cost-saving ideas in his company. Supervisors argue against the program because it doesn't increase the percentage of women and minorities in the company. In this case, the supervisors are invoking an irrelevant criterion.

The point is not that fairness to women and minorities is unimportant. Rather, fairness is a different issue and should not be made the measure of the reward program.

You can avoid the mistake of using irrelevant criteria. When you evaluate an idea, set aside all separate issues and agendas, no matter how important they are or how committed you feel about them.

Overgeneralizing or stereotyping

Generalizations are judgments about a class of people or things. Political pollsters are generalizing when they say, "Most voters don't care much about either presidential candidate." Though such a statement covers tens of millions of people, it's a fair one if based on a representative sample of those people.

Generalizations don't have to be based on a scientific sampling in order to be fair. They need only be based on a reasonable number of contacts with a reasonable number of people in the group. For example, your instructor might say, "My present students are more willing to participate in class than my students were last year." Or you could say, "The people in my neighborhood are friendly."

Overgeneralizations are unfair generalizations. They exceed what's appropriate to conclude from our experiences. Suppose a professor teaches only advanced French literature and sees only a small, unique group of students. If she says something about "the students at this college" based solely on her experience, she is thinking uncritically. Or consider a first-semester student who has contact with only five teachers. This person would be overgeneralizing if he judged "the faculty at this school."

Stereotypes are overgeneralizations that harden into convictions shared by many people. There are stereotypes of people: fundamentalists, politicians, feminists, psychiatrists, rock musicians. And there are stereotypes of places and things: New York City and San Francisco, marriage and farming.

Overgeneralizations and stereotypes hinder critical thinking by blinding us to important differences among individual people, places, and things.

Hasty conclusion

Hasty conclusions are those drawn without enough evidence. Consider this case: A student often leaves the door to his room open and many people have access to the room. One day he discovers an expensive pen is missing from his desk. He concludes that his roommate took it. This is a hasty conclusion. It's possible that his roommate stole the pen. It's also possible that someone else stole it. Or perhaps he lost or misplaced the pen.

In many cases, two or more conclusions are possible. Critical thinking means having a good reason for choosing one over the others. If no such reason exists, suspend judgment and seek more evidence.

Unwarranted assumption

Assumptions are ideas we take for granted. They differ from conclusions in an important way: We make assumptions unconsciously. They're implied rather than expressed.

There's nothing necessarily wrong with assumptions. Making them allows us to conduct our daily activities efficiently. When you got up this morning, you assumed there would be enough hot water to take a shower. If you drove to school, you probably assumed that your car would start and your instructors would hold classes. Unless there was a good reason not to make these assumptions—for example, if your water heater was broken—they would be valid.

The assumptions that hinder critical thinking are unwarranted assumptions. These occur when we take too much for granted. When this happens, we're prevented from asking useful questions and exploring possibilities.

Suppose someone assumes that it's the teacher's job to make a class interesting. That person is unlikely to ask herself, "What responsibility do the *students* have to create interesting classes?" That omission results from her unwarranted assumption. Here is another example:

Sally: You say that discrimination against women is a thing of the past. That's just not true.

Ralph: It certainly is true. I read it in a magazine.

Ralph has made a common unwarranted assumption: If something appears in print, it must be true. Notice that he hasn't said this. He may not even realize he's making any assumption. Nevertheless, he clearly implies it.

The fact that assumptions are unstated makes them hard to detect. When you look for assumptions in your own thinking and writing, go beyond what you consciously thought or wrote. Consider what you took for granted.

Failure to make a distinction

 Distinctions are subtle differences among things. Care in making distinctions can help you overcome confusion and deal with complex issues effectively. Following are some important distinctions to recognize.

The distinction between the person and the idea. Critical thinkers judge an idea on its own merits—not on the celebrity status or expertise of the person expressing it. Though experts usually have more informed views than novices, experts can be wrong and novices can have genuine insights.

The distinction between assertion and evidence. Some people pile assertion upon assertion without evidence. If these people are articulate, the casual thinker may be persuaded. Critical thinkers judge ideas on how well supported—and supportable—they are. This is more important than how well the idea is expressed.

The distinction between familiarity and validity. We're naturally attracted to the familiar. It's easy to believe that reasoning is valid merely because we've heard it many times. Critical thinkers, however, are not swayed by familiarity.

The distinction between often *and* always, seldom *and* never. Uncritical thinkers tend to ignore this distinction. They might say something "always" occurs when the evidence supports only "often," or they might say it "never" occurs when the evidence supports only "seldom." Critical thinkers are careful to make the distinction.

Oversimplification

There's nothing wrong with simplifying. In elementary school especially, teachers simplify their subjects. Professionals such as engineers and chemists simplify to communicate with people untrained in their fields.

Oversimplification differs from simplification. Oversimplification omits essential information or ignores complexity. Consider this idea: "High school teachers have it made. They're through at three o'clock every day and work only nine months of the year." Though there is some truth to this statement, it's inaccurate. Teachers often prepare four or five classes a day, grade homework, keep records, chaperone activities, and advise organizations. These activities often occur outside the normal eight-hour day. In addition, teachers are often required to take summer courses.

Oversimplification distorts reality and confuses discussion.

Exercise 50

Consider each of the seven errors of judgment. Think of times when you've committed them, and describe these situations. Explain how you reacted and what events followed. Then decide how you could have avoided each error and how the consequences might have been different.

Double standard

_____

_____

_____

_____

_____

_____

_____

Irrelevant criterion

_____

_____

_____

_____

_____

_____

Overgeneralizing or stereotyping

_____

_____

_____

_____

_____

_____

_____

Hasty conclusion

_____

_____

_____

_____

_____

_____

_____

Unwarranted assumption

_____

_____

_____

_____

_____

_____

_____

Failure to make a distinction

_____

_____

_____

_____

_____

_____

_____

Oversimplification

Exercise 51

Read each of the following passages carefully, looking for errors of
judgment. When you find one, explain the error in the space provided.

A.

Sue: My English instructor makes us rewrite any composition that contains more than three
errors in grammar or usage. And she's always demanding that we do better in our writing. I
think she dislikes us.

Ellen: I know what you mean. The professors at this college seem to think it's Harvard.

B.

Morris: Did you notice all the people using food stamps in the grocery store this morning?

Olaf: Yeah. It seems everybody has them these days. It's the fashionable thing to plead poverty.

Morris: That one woman was dressed well, too. I'll bet her lazy husband was waiting for her
outside in a big fancy car.

Olaf: It makes me sick, people like that leeching on society. Darwin had the right idea: survival of the fittest. If people can't survive on their own, let them suffer.

C.

Times change, and values in one age are different from values in another. Parents fail to realize this. That's why they keep harping about avoiding alcohol and drugs and postponing sexual involvement. They think that what was right for them is right for us.

_____

_____

_____

_____

_____

_____

D.

Boris: Can you believe the price of textbooks? The average amount I spent for a book this semester was $45, and a good half of my books are paperbacks.

Elaine: Everybody's complaining about it. When the cost of books keeps going up and up, there's only one explanation: The authors and publishers are getting greedy.

Boris: Yeah, and you know one of my instructors has the nerve to make us buy a book he wrote. And get this: He teaches Ethics!

Elaine: Wow.

_____

_____

_____

_____

_____

_____

E.

Zeb: Did you read the latest about Senator Fosdick? The candidate running against him claimed he knowingly received illegal campaign contributions.

Clarissa: How ironic. Senator Fosdick has been talking about campaign reform for years. Now it turns out he's as big a crook as the rest of them. What a hypocrite.

_____

_____

_____

_____

_____

_____

F.

Cynthia: A study has shown that as the speed limit has been raised, there's been an increase in traffic fatalities.

Mark: Speed limits don't cause traffic fatalities. Careless drivers do.

_____

_____

_____

_____

_____

_____

G.

Abdul: Any athlete who physically attacks his coach shouldn't just receive a fine. He should be arrested and charged with assault.

Simon: I disagree. No player attacks a coach without good reason. Besides, coaches are too negative, telling players what to do and yelling at them when they make mistakes. That behavior invites physical attack.

_____

_____

_____

_____

_____

_____

Errors of reaction

Errors of reaction occur when we express a viewpoint and someone reacts negatively. They are defensive reactions that preserve our self-image and provide an excuse to maintain our view. The following errors of reaction are the most common.

Explaining away

Ron has been a marijuana smoker for several years. He maintains that marijuana is harmless. Last night he and a group of friends were talking, and one of them mentioned that his health instructor had distributed an article from the *Journal of the American Medical Association*.

That article reported the results of a clinical study of marijuana use. It concluded that "contrary to what is frequently reported, we have found the effect of marijuana to be not merely that of a mild intoxicant which causes a slight exaggeration of usual adolescent behavior, but a specific and separate clinical syndrome." The main effects the study noted were "disturbed awareness of the self, apathy, confusion and poor reality testing."

Ron's reply was heated. "Those articles are written by a bunch of pansies who never smoked a joint. They're guessing, fantasizing, or worse, making up scare stories for parents to feed their kiddies. I've smoked pot for years, and I can tell you it's had no effect on me."

Ron found the prospect of being wrong about marijuana and the possibility of injuring himself too unpleasant to consider. This is understandable. Still, critical thinking would suggest that he at least read the article and examine the evidence. Instead, he resorted to a tactic long used in uncritical thinking: explain it away.

When people explain away challenges to their ideas, they don't change reality. They just postpone dealing with it. The longer they postpone, the more painful the experience. If you wish to avoid such results, face unpleasant ideas directly and honestly.

Shifting the burden of proof

Accepting the burden of proof means supporting our assertions. The more the assertions challenge accepted wisdom, the greater the burden. What's more, this burden falls on the person who makes the assertion. Here's how this concept applies in an actual case. Two students are discussing greatness in boxing:

Zeke: Mike Tyson was the greatest heavyweight boxer of all time.

Brad: Wait a minute. There have been a lot of great heavyweights over the years. I doubt Tyson was better than all of them.

Zeke: I stand by my position. Prove me wrong if you can.

There would be nothing wrong with Zeke's asking Brad why he doubts Tyson's greatness. But when Zeke says "Prove me wrong," he's shifting the burden of proof. Since Zeke made the original statement, he should be prepared to defend it.

When you make an assertion, you might be called on to defend it. And if you find that you can't defend the assertion, avoid shifting your burden of proof. Withdraw the assertion.

Attacking the person

In uncritical thinking there's a common way of reacting to challenges: attack the challenger. Here's a common scenario.

Melissa argues that it makes no sense for students to vote while they're away at college. The process of obtaining an absentee ballot is time consuming, she says. And with so many people voting, a student's vote isn't that important.

Agnes challenges Melissa's view. "I voted by absentee ballot last year," she says, "and the process was simple." Agnes adds that some elections are close enough to be decided by a few thousand votes. What's more, hundreds of thousands of college students are eligible to vote.

Now Melissa is embarrassed. The weakness of her view has been exposed in front of other students. She launches an attack on Agnes. "You have no business lecturing me about right and wrong. Just last week you cut Friday's classes so you could go home early, and then you lied to your instructors about being sick. Stop being a hypocrite, Agnes."

Even if this attack on Agnes is true, it has nothing to do with the issue of college students voting. It's merely a way for Melissa to save face.

How would Melissa respond if she practiced critical thinking? She would focus on Agnes's idea rather than on Agnes as a person. And since the idea seems reasonable, Melissa would probe it further before dismissing it. She could say, "Perhaps I'm mistaken. What steps are needed to vote by absentee ballot?" Then if Agnes's answer showed that the process was simple, Melissa could respond, "I guess you're right."

By acting this way, Melissa would not lose face. In fact, the other students might have been impressed at her flexibility and willingness to admit a mistake.

Straw man

As its name suggests, this error involves make-believe. Specifically, the error means pretending someone has said something that she has not said, and then denouncing her for saying it.

Imagine this situation. Someone has proposed that your school's attendance policy be revised to permit unlimited absences from class without penalty. You argue against the proposal, claiming that students who attend class sporadically slow the pace of learning for others and degrade the quality of class discussion.

Then someone responds to your argument as follows: "I take exception to your view. You say that adults should be treated as children, that students must leave their constitutional rights at the college gate, and that individuals whose work obligations sometimes force them to miss class are inferior creatures deserving of punishment."

Those stirring words, which bear no relation to reality, constitute the error of straw man. They attribute to you something you did not say. To avoid the error of straw man, listen to or read others' arguments carefully. Focus your criticism on what was actually said or clearly implied.

In all these errors of reaction, ego gets in the way of critical thinking. It's in your long-term interest to acknowledge error and learn from it. Doing so promotes knowledge and wisdom.

Exercise 52

Consider each of the four errors of reaction. Think of times when you committed them and describe these situations. Explain how you reacted and what consequences resulted. Then decide how you might have avoided the error and how the consequences might have been different. (If you can't think of an error of your own, identify one you encountered through reading or observation.)

Explaining away

_____

_____

_____

_____

_____

_____

_____

Shifting the burden of proof

_____

_____

_____

_____

_____

_____

_____

Attacking the person

_____
_____
_____
_____
_____
_____
_____

Straw man

_____
_____
_____
_____
_____
_____
_____

Practicing Critical Thinking 12

Add your thoughtful reflection on the following observation in the space provided.

Observation

Psychologist Abraham Maslow explained the hierarchy of human needs by using the figure of a pyramid (*see illustration*). The lower needs, he believed, must be met before the higher needs are pursued. At the bottom of his pyramid are physiological needs (food, clothing, shelter). Then comes the need for belongingness and love. Above that comes self-esteem, then aesthetic and intellectual needs. At the top, representing the highest need, is self-actualization.

Self-actualization

Aesthetic and intellectual needs

The need for self-esteem

Belongingness and love

Physiological needs (food, clothing, shelter)

Austrian psychiatrist Viktor Frankl challenged this order. He argued that self-transcendence—forgetting about self and seeking challenging tasks to add meaning to one's existence—is the highest human need. He also believed that self-actualization cannot be pursued but comes only by achieving self-transcendence. Several decades have passed since these two views were first presented, and in the United States Maslow's has been more influential.

Reflection

_____

_____

_____

_____

_____

_____

_____

Practicing Critical Thinking 13

Add your thoughtful reflection on the following observation in the space provided.

Observation

Many people reason that because everyone has a right to his or her opinion, everyone's opinion should be treated with respect and never challenged or disputed.

Reflection

_____

_____

_____

_____

_____

_____

Practicing Critical Thinking 14

In Practicing Critical Thinking 8 in Chapter Two you listed a number of observations to be examined more closely later. Look back at that list, select one of those observations, and restate it on a separate sheet of paper. Then follow the appropriate guide to reflection:

a) If you chose an *issue,* identify the various views people take on it and the evidence they offer in support of those views. Look for additional evidence and decide which view of the issue is most reasonable.

b) If you chose a *statement that seemed insightful,* think of appropriate ways to test the statement. Carry out the test(s) and decide whether the statement really is insightful.

c) If you chose a *statement that you suspected was shallow or mistaken* because it was at odds with your experience, think of ways to test the statement. Then carry out the test(s) and decide whether the statement really is *shallow or mistaken.*

d) If you chose a *matter that you wished to understand more fully,* do the necessary research and record what you learn.

Practicing Critical Thinking 15

On a separate piece of paper list your most recent observations in each of the following categories. (Save this list for a later assignment.)

a) Interesting issues you would like to address when you have more time

b) Statements that appear to be unusually insightful (they may have been made by authors, instructors, fellow students, or someone else)

c) Statements that seem shallow or mistaken

d) Anything you have experienced or heard about that you wish to understand more fully such as an incident, a process, or a procedure

Errors can multiply

Errors would be costly enough if they occurred singly and separately. Yet in many cases one error invites another and that leads to several more. It's natural for us to want knowledge and wisdom. (Have you ever met anyone who *wanted* to be ignorant and foolish?) And with only a small investment of imagination, people can go from wanting it to pretending they have it and from there to seeing the world in a self-serving way.

The resulting errors of perception pave the way for errors of judgment. Examples are jumping to conclusions that flatter our viewpoint, assuming too much, or ignoring important distinctions. And once we embrace errors of judgment, express them to others, and hear them criticized, we are tempted to commit errors of reaction to save face.

Remembering the ways in which errors tend to multiply can keep you motivated to think critically.

Name _____ Date _____ /_____ /_____

1 Explain each of the following terms and describe how the type of error
affects the thinking process: errors of perception, errors of judgment, errors
of reaction.

2 Define each of the following errors, explain when it occurs in the thought
process, and give an example of it. Use different examples from those in the text.

Double standard

Shifting the burden of proof

Unwarranted assumption

"Mine is better" thinking

Gullibility and skepticism

Irrelevant criterion

Pretending to know

Attacking the person

Oversimplification

Bias for or against change

Straw man

Explaining away

Selective perception

Hasty conclusion

Overgeneralizing or stereotyping

Failure to make a distinction

Bias toward the majority or the minority

Either/or thinking

Answers to this quiz may be found at http://college.hmco.com.

6

Applying Critical Thinking

Rthinking criticaLLy about esearch

T he word *research* refers to the data produced by investigation. To think critically about your research means simply to assess the information you obtain.

Previous chapters touched on this topic. Chapter One, for example, demonstrated how to test opinions and evaluate evidence. And Chapter Three explained how to conduct research. This section extends those discussions.

As noted earlier, Francis Bacon argued that the purpose of reading is neither to accept nor reject what is said but, instead, to weigh and consider it.

When that statement was first presented, you may have wondered, "Why is Bacon's observation considered a great insight? It seems rather obvious."

The work you have done in this book since then has probably answered the question for you. Bacon was stating the obvious because it needed stating. That is, because the temptation *not* to weigh and consider information is powerful. That temptation is caused by one or more of these biases:

Bias toward what confirms our views. We tend to be protective of our opinions. This is true whether we reason them out or borrow them mindlessly from others. Whenever we encounter information that confirms one of our opinions, our automatic reaction is to accept it. Similarly, we tend to reject information that challenges our opinion.

Bias toward familiar ideas. Suppose you walked into a cafeteria and had the choice of sitting with people you know or with strangers. Which would you choose? No doubt people you know because you'd feel more relaxed and comfortable with them. It's the same way with ideas. All of us tend to be more accepting of ideas we've heard before than we are of new ideas.

Bias toward what we like. We all have our personal preferences. There's nothing wrong with that. The problem arises only when we let them interfere with our judgment. If someone shares your taste in television programming, you may see her as a person of great wisdom and taste. In contrast, anyone who speaks critically of your favorite programming may seem an ignoramus.

All three biases are most dangerous when they are not blatant but subtle. That is when they can corrupt your thinking without your being aware.

Let's say you just read an article pointing out the deficiencies of home schooling. Most parents who home school, the author says, are not trained teachers, and some have not even graduated from college. In addition, he points out that even if the parent is a certified teacher, she is not likely to be skilled in art, music, *and* foreign language; nor will she be able to provide a lab science experience at home. Finally, the author argues that children who are home schooled are deprived of opportunities for socializing with peers. Thus, in his view, they are woefully unprepared to relate to people of other religions and cultures.

Now suppose that you know little about home schooling other than what you just read. Also, that you graduated from public school, feel generally positive about your experience there, and therefore support public education.

Having never taken a firm stand against home schooling, you'd probably consider yourself completely unbiased. That self-assessment would not be completely accurate. It would be more correct to say that you are mildly and subtly biased. And that slight, almost imperceptible tilt toward one side of the issue could prompt you to accept what the author says uncritically.

However, if you were more sensitive to your bias and made yourself examine the issue more fully, you would find that all the evidence is not against home schooling. You'd learn that creative home schoolers have discovered ways to overcome or compensate for the lack of laboratories and other limitations. In addition, you'd find that home schooled students often score as well as, and in some cases better than, public and private school graduates. Also, that there is no solid evidence that they have any problem working and living with people of other religions, races, and ethnic backgrounds.

The key to maintaining a critical perspective on your research is to prevent your biases from affecting your judgment. The best way to do that is to keep the following facts in mind.

Some information sources are unreliable

The communications/entertainment media often present opinions from people whose celebrity exceeds their competency. Some time ago a television interviewer asked an actress, "Did your role in that television drama give you any insights into adoption fraud?" (That's about as sensible as asking an actor who played a surgeon how to perform an appendectomy, or asking an actor who played an auto mechanic how to overhaul an engine.) Not surprisingly, the actress did not hesitate to offer her opinion, and millions of people mistakenly thought they were receiving meaningful information.

Other people decide what you should know

Suppose that you open today's newspaper and the front page headlines say that Reverend Jesse Jackson led a protest march, Israelis and Arabs clashed in Palestine, and a snowstorm blanketed the midwest.

Like many people, you may take it for granted that those stories represent the most important events that occurred in the past 24 hours. But stop and think about that. The editors who selected those stories have their own ideas of what is newsworthy. And their ideas may be debatable. For example, many editors follow the principle, "If it bleeds, it leads," and it could be argued that this principle distorts reality.

Consider, as well, this fact: In choosing those stories, the editors also chose to ignore many other stories. For example, did you read about the historic conference in Washington, D.C., featuring a Catholic priest, a Protestant minister, a Black Muslim, a Hindu, a Rabbi, and a Buddhist talking about their common spiritual and social values? (This event took place in November 2000.) Chances are you didn't hear about it because most editors around the country decided it wasn't newsworthy.

The same pattern exists in book and magazine publishing. Authors are free to take any view they want about any subject. But what the editors select for publication is what they think the public should know.

Some presentations are less than honest

This is particularly, but not exclusively, true of political statements. Former presidential advisor Dick Morris says political candidates' speeches are like collections of "greatest hits." They say what polls and test groups suggest people want to hear. That's why words such as *trust, family,* and *values* are used so commonly (*60 Minutes,* July 4, 1999).

New research sometimes overturns prior conclusions

Not long ago research demonstrated that fiber lowers cholesterol and protects against colon cancer. However, later research proved that it doesn't lower cholesterol. Then additional research showed that it doesn't protect against colon cancer (*Consumer Reports on Health,* August 1999, 1). So it's not enough to consult some scientific studies—we've got to be sure they're up to date.

Your opinion could be wrong

We all make mistakes from time to time. The sooner we find out we've made one, the better off we are. And the best way to find a mistake early is to be open to ideas that challenge our own.

Familiarity is coincidental

The order in which we hear ideas and the frequency of our hearing them are matters of chance. The fact that we've heard something repeated a dozen times doesn't mean it is any more reliable than something we are hearing for the first time. For this reason, it's foolish to attach any significance to familiarity.

Your likes and dislikes are being manipulated

The advertising industry has long been playing mind games with us. TV viewers typically see more than 64,000 commercials *annually,* each one cleverly designed to make viewers like something enough to buy it. Similar marketing devices are used to get people to watch one TV program rather than another and to support one political candidate rather than his or her opponent.

The crucial question to ask about your likes and dislikes is, "Are these really mine or have I been tricked into adopting them?"

Do you find any of these facts disturbing? That is a healthy reaction. Keep all of them in mind as you do the exercises in this and subsequent chapters, as well as when you deal with issues in everyday life.

Exercise 53

Note your immediate reaction to each of the following issues. Then reflect on that reaction and determine what your bias is. Be especially alert for subtle bias. State your findings and explain what you could do to prevent your bias from affecting your judgment. (You do not have to conduct any analysis.)

a) In Louisiana schools, students are required to address teachers as "sir" or "ma'am." Is this requirement reasonable?

_____

_____

_____

_____

_____

_____

_____

_____

b)   *Does there tend to be a liberal bias about political and social issues in TV reporting and commentary?*

_____

_____

_____

_____

_____

_____

_____

_____

_____

c)   *Are boys or girls more favored in today's schools?*

_____

_____

_____

_____

_____

_____

_____

_____

_____

C Thinking criticaLLy about ommercials

A dvertisers spend billions of dollars a year on commercials. The cost of just one 15-second commercial can exceed $500,000. In many cases advertising goes beyond presenting the product or service. Advertisers stimulate viewers through appeals to desires: to be youthful, sexually appealing, successful, loved, or accepted by others. In advertising language, the aim is to "sell the sizzle, not the steak."

Former advertising executive Jerry Mander claims that advertising exists only to create needs for products. The trick, he says, is to make people feel discontented. And the standard advertising formula for doing so is to (1) gain the audience's attention, (2) arouse their interest, (3) stimulate a desire for the product, and (4) make the sales pitch.

The design of a commercial (or print ad), Mander explains, is no casual affair. Advertisers employ thousands of psychologists, behavioral scientists, perception researchers, and sociologists. These experts identify deep-seated human needs and desires, insecurities and fears. Then they determine how these can be used to the advertiser's advantage.

The techniques of advertising are the techniques of propaganda. Among the most common are the following:

Bandwagon

This technique creates the impression that everyone is buying the product or service. It appeals to the viewer's urge to conform.

Glittering generality

Here the advertiser uses words and phrases to imply excellence and uniqueness. Few specifics are offered. "Amazing new discovery," "now a stunning breakthrough," and "unheard-of softness" are examples of glittering generality.

Empty comparison

This technique uses words such as *better, bigger,* and *more* (as in "more economical") without completing the comparison. What, for example, does "greater cleaning power" mean? Greater than last year? Greater than the competition? Such a statement seems to make a serious claim. And yet we can't hold the advertiser responsible for it because we aren't sure just what is being claimed.

Meaningless slogan

Most large companies have slogans designed to create a positive impression. These create pleasant images but promise little.

United Airlines' slogan, "Fly the friendly skies," was designed to associate that airline with friendliness. "AT&T—The Right Choice" tried to link the act of choosing a telephone company with AT&T. Another slogan is "Michelin . . . because so much is riding on your tires," and with these words we see pictures of adorable babies. The aim: to have viewers associate buying Michelin tires with protecting their children.

Testimonial

A testimonial is an endorsement for a product or a service. Actors, musicians, sports figures, and other well-known people are paid substantial sums of money to appear in commercials, lending their credibility and celebrity status to products. The words they speak may be written by someone else, and viewers often know this. Even so, advertisers still hope we'll associate the celebrity with the product or service.

Transfer

One common kind of transfer is the voice-over. Here the celebrity never appears in the commercial but acts as off-camera narrator. Even if the viewer cannot name the speaker, the voice may be familiar and make the message more appealing.

Another kind of transfer involves objects instead of people. For example, the Statue of Liberty or the flag could be shown with a product or service. These symbols arouse strong positive feelings in many people. Advertisers want viewers to transfer those feelings to the product.

A less obvious use of transfer is the "party scene," in which we see people enjoying themselves. The intended message is that the featured product—a beer or wine cooler—made the occasion enjoyable.

The standard commercial break consists of four 15-second commercials. The average number of commercials in an hour of television viewing is 44. If you watch four hours of television a day you encounter 176 appeals designed to short-circuit your critical thinking and create an artificial desire or need. Your best safeguard against this manipulation is to use your critical thinking skills.

Stacking the deck

This technique is often used when comparisons are made between the advertiser's product and a competitor's product. For example, one commercial showed a competitor's fish sticks on a cookie sheet, all in black and white, looking as if they were still frozen. Then the scene shifted to the advertiser's frozen dinner appetizingly presented in vibrant color, with steam rising.

A similar approach is used in many diet commercials. For example, a "before" picture will be a fuzzy black and white print, with the person dressed poorly and looking sad. In contrast, the "after" picture will be sharply focused, in color, and with the person well dressed and happy.

Misleading statement

This technique uses words that invite viewers to make an erroneous interpretation. Such statements appear to promise something but in reality do not. Lately a number of long distance telephone ads use such statements.

One such commercial promises "8¢ a minute for calls over ten minutes. That's a 50% saving." That invites thinkers to conclude that they will save 50% on every call. But the ad does not say what calls under ten minutes cost. Is it 8¢? 18¢? 28¢? We can't be sure.

Another commercial says we can talk up to twenty minutes for 99¢. We're tempted to think that's a rate of less than 5¢ a minute. But wait. If the 99¢ is a flat rate, then a five-minute call would cost almost 20¢ a minute and a two-minute call would cost almost 50¢! That's quite a difference.

Exercise 54

Watch at least two hours of television. Pay close attention to the commercials. For this assignment the programs themselves are unimportant. If you wish, do some other activity between commercial breaks.

As you observe each commercial, note the product or service advertised, the scenes shown, and the people on camera. Also listen for the narrator, music, and other sounds.

Next, select three of the commercials you observed. On a separate sheet of paper, describe each commercial and then analyze it by answering the following questions:

- Does the commercial motivate the viewers to think or merely appeal to their emotions? Explain.
- What hopes, fears, or desires is the commercial designed to exploit? How?
- What attitudes and values does the commercial promote—for example, attitudes about success and happiness? How does the commercial promote them? Do you share these attitudes and values?

- Does the commercial use propaganda techniques? How?
- Would you classify this commercial as fair or unfair persuasion? What's the evidence for your view?

Exercise 55

Calculate the average attention shifts occurring during commercials. Proceed as follows.

Watch any half-hour or hour program. When a commercial break occurs, keep your eyes focused on the television set. Each time a new image appears on the screen, make a tally on the page. (Use a separate sheet of paper for this tally.) When the next commercial appears, resume your tally on a new line.

At the end of the program, divide the number of lines into the grand total of stroke tallies. The answer will be the average attention shifts occurring during commercials for that program.

Summarize your findings in the space provided and then answer the following questions:

Number of tallies (images) ———

Number of lines (commercials) ———

Average attention shifts during the commercials ———

Were you surprised at the number of attention shifts per commercial? Explain.

_____

_____

_____

_____

_____

What possible reasons might advertising agencies have for changing images at that rate? Which of those reasons seems most likely? Explain.

_____

_____

_____

_____

Television commercials in the 1950s and 1960s were one minute long and contained relatively few images. Typically, one or more people talked about the product as they displayed it. In the 1970s and 1980s commercials were 30 seconds long and contained more images.

Today's commercials are 15 seconds in length and contain considerably more images. What effect, if any, could this change have had on academic performance? Job performance? Personal relationships? Explain your thoughts carefully.

_____

_____

_____

_____

_____

_____

_____

Exercise 56

On the basis of your analyses in Exercises 54 and 55, do you think the Federal Communications Commission should change the standards for commercials? What restrictions, if any, should they impose? On a separate sheet of paper, write a composition of at least several paragraphs supporting your view. (You may wish to consult the guidelines in Chapter Seven, "Expressing Ideas Persuasively.")

Practicing Critical Thinking 16

If you watch television, you've probably encountered some or all of the commercial slogans shown below. Reflect on these slogans individually, or as a group, in light of this and previous chapters.

"Just do it." (Nike slogan)

_____

_____

_____

"Image is everything." (Canon slogan)

_____

_____

_____

"Life is short—play hard." (Reebok slogan)

_____

_____

_____

"On planet Reebok there are no rules."

_____

_____

_____

"Why ask why? Try Bud Dry." (Budweiser slogan)

_____

_____

_____

Voice asks, *"What should I drink?"* Narrator says,
"Give your brain a rest. Try some Sprite."

_____

_____

_____

*"Though we carry over 160,000 passengers a day, we serve
each of them one at a time."* (USAirways slogan)

_____

_____

_____

"Red Wolf is here. Follow your instincts."
(Red Wolf beer slogan)

_____

_____

_____

"We measure success one investor at a time."
(Dean Witter slogan)

_____

_____

_____

Pthinking criticaLLy about
rint advertising

Like television commercials, print advertising is designed to sell a product, a service, or an idea. Such advertising may appeal to the desire for happiness or the need for belonging, acceptance, or love. However, the techniques that print ads use are more limited. They cannot use sound or depict motion. They are strictly visual and static.

Advertisers know how to make a print ad effective. Every detail must contribute to the overall message. They take great care in choosing every word and picture.

Analyzing print ads involves studying these choices.

Always ask yourself whether the statements made in print ads make sense. Suppose an auto ad says, "Due to unprecedented demand, we are discounting hundreds of cars in our lot." But think about it. If the demand were high, the prices wouldn't be changed. The reality must be that *too few people* are buying.

Also read the fine print. No doubt you've gotten more than one credit card ad that says: "Why pay an adjustable rate of 17.9% or 18.9% when you can pay a low FIXED rate of only 4.9%?" That certainly sounds like a great deal . . . until you look at the fine print and learn that the rate is "fixed" for three months. And after that? Presumably the sky's the limit.

Look critically at the pictures in print ads, too. Their effect can be even more powerful than words. Cigarette ads have been especially clever in depicting smokers as physically attractive people having a wonderful time as they puff.

Other ads are equally clever. A perfume ad pictured a man and a woman in a highly aroused state. The caption read, "Unleash your fantasies." The unspoken promise was that using the perfume would heighten sexual fulfillment.

Some ads are truly offensive. Another perfume ad showed a beautiful but frightened woman with several men clinging to her. The caption read "No one could protect her from herself." And a jeans ad showed a woman being backed into a fence by cowboys. The implied meaning of these ads was that women enjoy being assaulted.

Some critics say most advertising is dishonest at best. They are especially troubled by the ads directed at the most vulnerable individuals, children. Defenders of advertising deny the charge, claiming that advertising is simply honest persuasion.

Exercise 57

Visit the magazine section of your campus library. Skim at least a half-dozen magazines, looking for interesting print ads. Don't limit yourself to magazines you already know. The wider your assortment, the more varied the ads you'll find. Next, select two ads and describe each one. Then analyze them by answering the questions below. If you wish, attach a photocopy of the ads.

- Does the advertisement motivate the viewers to think or merely appeal to their emotions? Explain.
- What hopes, fears, or desires, if any, is the ad designed to exploit? How does it appeal to them?
- What attitudes or values, if any, does the ad promote—for example, attitudes about success? How does it promote them?
- Do you share those attitudes and values?
- What propaganda techniques, if any, are used? Explain how they are used.
- Would you classify this ad as fair or unfair persuasion? What's the evidence for your view?

First ad

Description:

_____

_____

_____

Analysis:

_____

_____

_____

Second ad

Description:

_____

_____

_____

Analysis:

_____

_____

_____

Thinking criticaLLy about Television programming

By high school graduation the average person has spent 11,000 hours in the classroom and 22,000 hours watching television. All things being equal, television has twice as much impact on a person's mind as formal education.

Yet all things are not equal. Television producers have more means to maintain audience attention. They can use music to manipulate emotions. Directors can shift scenes to sustain interest and use applause tracks to cue responses. All this is evidence for television's impact. The question continues to be debated: Is that impact mainly positive or negative?

In 1961 Newton Minow, then chairman of the Federal Communications Commission, called television a "vast wasteland." Twenty-five years later his judgment was essentially the same. In Minow's view and those of other critics, television seriously underestimates the viewer's intelligence.

Other critics of television programming argue that it also creates mental habits and attitudes that hinder learning. These critics advance the following arguments:

- By keeping young people away from books, television denies them opportunities to develop imagination.

- Television aims programming at the lowest common denominator. This deprives young people of intellectual challenge.

- By feeding young people a steady diet of slang and clichés, television hinders their language skills.

- Television limits game show questions to who? what? where? and when?—seldom how? and never why? This creates the impression that knowledge of trivia is the only knowledge worth having. It also implies that careful analysis of issues is unnecessary or boring.

- Television uses the narrative approach for most of its programming. Examples are soap operas, sitcoms, movies, and dramatic series. By doing so, television denies young people exposure to critical thinking. (Such thinking is more commonly expressed in analysis than in narrative.)

■ Television fills the roster of talk shows with celebrities rather than authorities. By doing so, television creates the impression that it's not what you know but how well you are known that's important.

Jerry Mander has analyzed why television has failed to live up to expectations. In *Four Arguments for the Elimination of Television,* he claims that television has a number of inherent limitations that cannot easily be overcome. For one thing, it is an artificial environment that viewers have no hand in creating. Even on newscasts, we see only what others decide to show us, and always from their particular perspective and according to their priorities. For every item included in the news, thousands are excluded.

Another limitation is that less dramatic things don't play as well on television as more dramatic ones. That is why we see more angry expressions than happy ones, more fistfights and shootings than calm discussions, more car chases and explosions than tranquil scenes, more passionate sexual encounters than gentler expressions of friendship, caring, and tenderness.

A third limitation, according to Mander, is that the everyday pace of reality is not well suited to television. To make their stories interesting, programmers have to compress events. TV heroes are confronted by one dangerous situation after another, whereas in real life many tedious hours of inactivity intervene. Regular television viewing can create the unrealistic expectation that real life ought to be one peak experience after another.

The expectation is reinforced by the news. Reporters prefer to cover sensational stories. When they are forced to cover an ordinary event they often seek out the most dramatic or sensational aspect—for example, the single angry outburst in an otherwise calm and productive city council meeting. Antisocial behavior is deemed more newsworthy than social behavior.

The inherent limitations of television result in a number of biases in selecting program material. Mander finds more than 30, including the following:

A bias for war over peace, and violence over nonviolence

A bias for superficiality over depth, simplification over balance

A bias for feelings of conflict over feelings of agreement

A bias for dissatisfaction over satisfaction, anger over tranquility, jealousy over acceptance

A bias for competition over cooperation

A bias for materialism over spirituality

A bias for the bizarre over the commonplace, the fixed over the evolutionary, the static over the dynamic

If these charges by Mander and others are valid, television may be responsible for a number of social problems. For example, it may cause or aggravate many of the difficulties students experience in school, some of which cause them to drop out before graduating. Television may also be responsible for the tendency of many people to settle for mediocrity rather than strive for excellence.

The following exercises direct your critical thinking to these questions: Is television programming harming our country and its citizens? If so, what can be done to correct that? If not, what can be done to make television programming an even more positive influence?

Exercise 58

Select a television game show and watch it for one or more programs. Note the way the game is played, the kinds of questions asked, and the time allowed for responses. Also note background effects such as music, lights, or revolving wheels and any other significant details about the show. Then analyze what you've seen. Answer these and any other relevant questions:

■ How intellectually demanding is the show?

_____

_____

_____

■ What is the show's appeal to viewers?

_____

_____

_____

■ What habits or attitudes could this show develop or reinforce in regular adult viewers? In children? Will these habits and attitudes help or hinder life in school, on the job, and at home?

_____

_____

_____

_____

Next, on a separate sheet of paper write a composition of at least several paragraphs. Explain and support your reactions.

Exercise 59

Select a television sitcom and watch it for one or more programs. Then analyze what you saw. Answer these and other relevant questions:

■ How original was the story line? Can you remember any other show you've seen with a similar plot?

_____

_____

_____

■ What attitudes and values did the show encourage? Do you share them?

_____

_____

_____

■ Did the characters rise above stereotypes: the dumb blonde, the know-it-all teenagers, and so on?

_____

_____

■ Would you have laughed if the show had had no laugh track? How original were the jokes?

_____

_____

Next, on a separate sheet of paper, write a composition of at least several paragraphs. Explain and support your reactions.

Exercise 60

Choose a television drama—a soap opera, detective or western show, or a movie. To help yourself think critically, pick a show you don't normally see. Watch the show and then analyze what you saw. Answer these and any other relevant questions:

■ Which characters did the show present favorably? What was the main action taken by each of those characters during the show?

_____

_____

_____

■ Think about the characters you chose in the above question. What view would each express on the following topics?

Reasoning with others:

_____

_____

_____

Violence:

_____

_____

_____

Sexual relationships:

_____

_____

_____

Marriage:

_____

_____

_____

Authority:

_____

_____

_____

Success:

_____

_____

_____

■ Did the show include any incidents of violence and/or destruction? If so, describe them and explain whether their depiction was essential to the plot.

■ Were people or principles betrayed during the show? If so, describe each incident and explain whether the betrayal was presented in a positive or a negative light.

_____

_____

_____

_____

_____

■ Did the show emphasize antagonism or harmony? Were issues resolved peacefully or violently? Explain.

_____

_____

_____

_____

On a separate sheet of paper write a composition of at least several paragraphs, based on your analysis. Explain whether the show you watched promoted desirable attitudes and habits.

Exercise 61

Skim the television talk show listings. Then select a show and watch it. Analyze what you saw, answering these and any other relevant questions:

■ What was the show's theme or discussion topic?

_____

_____

■ What fields did the guests represent: show business, education, particular professions, or others? Are the guests associated with specific attitudes, values, behaviors? If so, describe those attitudes, values, or behaviors.

_____

_____

_____

■ What was the reason why each appeared on the show? For example, an author may have published a new book or an actress may have starred in a just-released film.

_____

_____

_____

■ What kinds of questions did the host ask? Professional questions? Personal questions?

_____

_____

_____

■ Were any specific attitudes and values encouraged? If so, what were they? Do you share them?

_____

_____

_____

■ How much time did the host allow for each answer? Did the guest have an opportunity to elaborate on answers? How much time was devoted to each guest?

_____

_____

_____

■ How many times was the discussion interrupted by commercial breaks?

_____

_____

_____

Next, write a composition of at least several paragraphs on a separate sheet of paper. Focus on this question: Would regular viewing of talk shows like the one you watched be good preparation for the probing discussions conducted in college classrooms?

Exercise 62

Watch the evening newscasts on PBS and one of the following: CNN, CBS, NBC, ABC. Compare their presentations of the news. Answer these and any other relevant questions:

■ How much time, on average, was given to each news story?

_____

_____

_____

■ What details did the newscasters focus on? What questions did they pass over? Did you want answers to any of the latter questions?

_____

_____

_____

■ How were the newscasts similar? Look, for example, at the numbers and genders of the newscasters, construction of the studio sets, and each show's format. How were the shows different?

_____

_____

_____

■ How many commercial breaks occurred during the newscast?

_____

_____

- Do you think the news stories gave a fair picture of world events?

_____

_____

_____

- What other types of stories might have been included?

_____

_____

_____

- Decide how the news broadcasts you watched could help or hinder intellectual development. Write a composition explaining and supporting your views.

_____

_____

_____

_____

_____

_____

_____

_____

_____

_____

_____

_____

_____

_____

_____

_____

_____

_____

_____

_____

_____

_____

_____

_____

Exercise 63

Consider the observations and judgments of the various kinds of television programming from the previous exercises. Decide what changes would improve television programming. Then write a letter to the Federal Communications Commission. State your ideas for improving programming and give reasons for acting on those ideas.

_____

_____

_____

_____

_____

_____

_____

_____

_____

_____

_____

_____

_____

_____

_____

_____

_____

_____

_____

_____

_____

_____

_____

_____

_____

M Thinking criticaLLy about ovies

Some people believe critical thinking has little application to movies because movies are an art form—representations of life designed to give pleasure rather than arguments offered to persuade people.

This view is an example of either/or thinking. It assumes that entertainment and persuasion are mutually exclusive. They are not. Moviemakers often want both to create a work of art *and* to influence people's thinking. In some cases, the persuasive intention takes precedence.

It is true that movies almost never present ideas directly in the manner of nonfiction writing. Nevertheless, ideas are embedded in the stories. Simply said, they show the ideas rather than tell them. The effect is more emotional than intellectual, but no less potent for that.

If a filmmaker wants to hold an idea up to ridicule, for example, he need only create a character who holds that idea and make her appear ridiculous.

In order to think critically about movies, you must understand the various elements. The basic ones are the same as those in short stories, novels, and plays.

Characters

Every story has one or more main characters, and often a number of secondary ones. The way the characters are presented will influence the audience's reaction to them.

Setting

The elements of setting are time, place, and the circumstances in which the story takes place.

Plot

The plot is the sequence of events that occurs in the story. The essential element in a movie plot is *conflict*. A challenge or problem confronts the characters and they struggle to solve it. The conflict may be external or merely within the character's mind.

Theme

The theme of a movie is the message or lesson it offers. The theme is almost never stated directly, though the dialogue may contain statements that clearly imply it.

In addition to the basic elements, movies have three other elements not found in written literature—the performances of the actors, sound effects, and visual effects. Sound effects include background music as well as dialogue. Visual effects are created by moving the camera in for closeup shots or out for distance shots, as well as by varying the lighting and camera angles.

In thinking critically about movies, it is important to evaluate each of the elements and make a balanced judgment. Seldom will a movie be uniformly excellent in all elements. The characters, for example, may be richly drawn and the plot plausible and ingenious. Yet the acting may be poor and the theme an insult to the viewer's intelligence.

The Golden Globe and Academy Awards reflect these distinctions. Rarely will a film "sweep" the awards. And even when it succeeds in doing so, or comes close, critical thinking will sometimes reveal serious weaknesses.

Consider, for example, the film that won a host of Academy Awards in the year 2000, *American Beauty*. (The awards included Best Picture, Best Actor, Best Screenplay, and Best Cinematography.)

The film is the story of Lester Burnam (played by Kevin Spacey) in the throes of a mid-life crisis. He quits his job, becomes obsessed with and nearly seduces his daughter's teenage girlfriend, and begins smoking marijuana purchased from his daughter's boyfriend. Only after he dies does he gain the (unoriginal) "insight" that our lives are quite small and insignificant compared to the vastness of the cosmos.

An overview of the characters reveals something many reviewers of the film overlooked. All four adults are seriously disturbed. Lester's neighbor is a homophobic Marine with secret homosexual urges. The neighbor's browbeaten wife is nearly catatonic. Lester's wife puts work above family and cheats on her husband with a fellow real estate agent, who is shallow and self-absorbed.

In contrast, all the teenagers are both pure of heart and wise. In fact, the drug pusher boyfriend has the controlling insight of the film, which Lester has to die to realize.

To sum up, *American Beauty* portrays adults as contemptible if not corrupt, especially those who represent discipline, order, and responsibility. Teenagers, on the other hand, are wonderful. Among the questions critical thinking raises about this film are these: Are the characterizations of adults and teenagers plausible? How reasonable is the theme?

Exercise 64

Select a movie you have recently seen; or, if you wish, rent a video and watch it. Then evaluate the film on a separate sheet of paper. Follow this format:
1. State the name of the film.
2. Identify the main and important secondary characters and the setting.
3. Explain the plot and identify what you believe to be the theme.
4. Judge the film's strengths and weaknesses.

M Thinking critically about usic

Ridiculing another generation's music has long been a popular pastime. Someone once defined an opera as a place where anything that is too dumb to be spoken is sung. Another person observed that classical music threatens to develop a tune with every other bar and then disappoints us. A third termed jazz an appeal to the emotions by an attack on the nerves. Another, writing of rock music, suggested that the proper pitch for most electrical guitars is right out the window, followed by the player.

Yet the fact that each generation prefers its own music does not mean that all criticism is without merit. It is important to keep this in mind in evaluating contemporary music.

Music has changed greatly in the past half-century, perhaps more so than in any comparable period in history. In the late 1940s two older musical traditions continued in vogue. One was Big Band music, played for ballroom dancing ranging from the elegant foxtrot to frenetic jitterbugging. The other was jazz.

The 1950s brought rock and roll with its very different beat, both literally and figuratively It may have lacked the refinement and style of jazz, but there was no doubting its raucous energy. From the days of Elvis Presley's "Blue Suede Shoes" to the present, rock and roll has undergone several transformations, notably to acid rock and then heavy metal. And other music forms have become popular—reggae, for example, and rap.

The differences between 1940s music and today's music go beyond the overall sound or the beat. Because no amplification existed then, the loudest jazz band was much quieter than today's groups. In those days, too, singers still crooned ballads in the manner of Bing Crosby and Frank Sinatra. Lyrics were meant to be understood and the singer's voice was regarded as another fine instrument to be used with precision to produce pleasant, melodious sounds. Singers wore hair styles no different from those of business people. All that has changed.

A more significant difference than these is the ideas and attitudes conveyed by the lyrics themselves and the mannerisms that accompany them. Today's lyrics and stage antics would have been unimaginable 50 years ago. Many popular videos celebrate the destruction of property, rape, child abuse, incest, sadism, murder, and suicide. Onscreen images depict these behaviors in graphic detail. And the average age of the audience that watches them is between 14 and 16.

Critics of contemporary music have charged that it is undermining the fundamental values of society and causing antisocial attitudes and behavior, including crime. Spokespeople for the music industry tend to dismiss such criticism, claiming that musicians are only exercising their right of free expression and no one can be harmed by that. The exercises that follow will give you an opportunity to examine this issue.

Exercise 65

Visit a music store and examine a number of current CDs or cassettes. Note the cover designs, song titles, and lyrics. Listen to releases from major groups. Then, on a separate sheet of paper, list each CD or cassette you examined and record your observations.

Exercise 66

Analyze your findings about the music you researched. Answer these and any other relevant questions:

■ On the basis of your inquiry, would you say the music conveys positive values and attitudes?

_____

_____

_____

_____

_____

_____

_____

■ Suppose that people applied the messages in the song lyrics to their lives. In what specific ways would their behavior be affected? Would the consequences be desirable or undesirable?

_____

_____

_____

_____

_____

_____

_____

■ Are the complaints against popular music justified? If not, why not? If so, what action
do you recommend? Who should take that action? Government? The music industry?

_____

_____

_____

_____

_____

_____

Now, present your view in a short composition. Include appropriate explanation and
support.

_____

_____

_____

_____

_____

_____

_____

_____

_____

_____

_____

_____

_____

_____

_____

_____

_____

_____

M Thinking criticaLLy about
agazines

Literally hundreds of magazines are available on a
variety of subjects, including animals, art, investment,
computers, entertainment, hob-
bies, home and garden, nature,
religion, science, and travel.
Among the most widely read
are news magazines such as
Time, Newsweek, and *U.S.
News and World Report.* Also
popular are the general interest tabloid magazines such as
People, The Star, and *The National Enquirer.*

Some magazines publish only staff-written articles. Others solicit articles from
freelance writers. Every magazine has its own specific areas of interest, format, editorial requirements, and point of view.

A magazine's target audience may be broad, as in the case of most news magazines, or narrow. There are magazines for political conservatives and magazines for
liberals, some for men and others for women. Age, marital status, and work status
are further areas of specialization. *McCall's,* for example, is published for women in
general; *Redbook,* for young mothers, ages 25–44; *Cosmopolitan,* for working
women, 18–35, who are single, married, or divorced.

Among the most common criticisms of news and/or general interest magazines
are the following:

- ■ The editorial biases of news magazines often result in a lack of objectivity in
reporting, particularly on issues related to bias. A secular bias, for example,
might prejudice the treatment of religion; a liberal political bias might prejudice the treatment of conservative proposals or programs.

- ■ General interest magazines often promote shallowness and superficiality by focusing on the details of celebrities' lives, particularly scandalous details.

- ■ Many magazines allow their choice and treatment of subject matter to be influenced—and often compromised—by their advertisers.

- ■ Many magazines tend to reinforce the values of popular culture—in particular,
impulsiveness, self-indulgence, and instant gratification—rather than the values
of traditional culture.

The following exercises invite you to apply critical thinking and decide whether these charges are valid. To complete these assignments you may decide to visit a newsstand, a library, or a bookstore.

Exercise 67

Examine the current editions of several news magazines—*Time, Newsweek, and U.S. News and World Report* or one written from a particular ethnic perspective. Select a single news item and compare the treatment it is given in each magazine. Decide which magazine's treatment is most biased and which is least biased. Support your findings.

Your decision and support:

_____

_____

_____

_____

_____

_____

_____

_____

Exercise 68

Check the covers of the current issues of magazines such as *Cosmopolitan, McCall's, Esquire, Redbook,* and *Psychology Today.* (Feel free to include any other magazine to which you subscribe or in which you are interested.) Compare the titles of the articles listed on the covers. Do these titles raise any questions about the magazines' themes, focuses, or editorial perspectives? Explain your findings.

_____

_____

_____

_____

_____

_____

_____

Exercise 69

Examine an edition of each of the following publications: *The Star, The National Enquirer,* and *People.* Read the articles, the special sections, and the advice columns. Sample the ads and look closely at the photographs. Then answer these questions:

■ Suppose that a stranger to this country were to draw a conclusion about our society's attitudes and values just from reading these publications. What conclusion do you think she would draw? What about these periodicals makes you think so?

_____

_____

_____

_____

_____

_____

_____

■ Do you think these publications merely reflect our society's attitudes and values or do they also help shape those attitudes and values? Explain.

_____

_____

_____

_____

_____

_____

_____

■ What changes in format and emphasis would you recommend to improve these publications? On a separate sheet of paper, present your response in a composition of several paragraphs.

N Thinking criticaLLy about ewspapers

The newspaper is an ancient form of communication that can be traced back to about 59 B.C. when the Roman *Acta Diurna* was posted in public places. Its greatest development, however, occurred after the invention of printing in the fifteenth century. More recently, the invention of the telegraph, the photocomposition process, and the communications satellite have made news gathering and publication faster and more efficient.

Other inventions, however, have challenged the newspaper's position as the leading provider of information. The most notable of these inventions have been radio and television, and the personal computer has similar potential. All three make news available at the flip of a switch, whereas the newspaper is available, in most cases, only once a day and must be delivered.

The newspaper has a further disadvantage—it requires the effort of reading. In contrast, broadcast news is obtained effortlessly, and in a conveniently rapid pace, in moving pictures. In reaction to this handicap, the newspaper industry has simplified and shortened stories. The most extreme example of this approach is the *USA Today* format.

Another change in print journalism over the past few decades concerns the treatment of fact and opinion. Traditionally, news stories presented only facts, objectively and without comment. A special place was reserved for commentary—the op-ed page (the term is short for opinion-editorial). There the reader would find editorials presenting the newspaper's official point of view on issues of the day, letters expressing readers' reactions to previous news stories, and opinion essays written by professional columnists.

Today's newspapers still have op-ed pages, with editorials, letters, and columns. But opinion is no longer carefully screened out of news stories. Many journalists, in fact, blend their interpretations and personal judgments into the news. Only the alert reader will understand where reporting ends and editorializing begins.

The op-ed page is often the most rewarding part of the newspaper because it is filled with lively analysis of current issues. The following exercises invite you to apply your critical thinking skills to that page.

Exercise 70

Choose the largest newspaper in your area or a newspaper serving a larger audience, such as *USA Today.* Read the main editorial of the day. Also read any news story mentioned in the editorial. Then, on a separate sheet of paper, answer the following questions:

- What position does the editor take on the issue? What support does he or she offer for this position?
- What other positions could be taken on the issue? How might those positions be supported? Before answering these questions, you may wish to research the issue by visiting the library or interviewing experts.
- What are the editorial's strengths and weaknesses?
- What position is most reasonable in light of the evidence? Present your response in a composition of at least several paragraphs. Another option is to write your response as a letter to the editor. If you do this, consider sending the letter to the newspaper.

Exercise 71

Select an opinion column or a letter to the editor that interests you. Examine it critically. If appropriate, research the issue further. Then, on a separate piece of paper, write a composition of at least several paragraphs stating and supporting your position on the issue. You may agree with the article or letter in the newspaper, disagree with it, or agree in part. Attach either a summary or a copy of the original article or letter.

Practicing Critical Thinking 17

Reflect on the following observation on a separate sheet of paper. Decide if the observation is significant, and if so, in what way.

Observation
In a District of Columbia study some years ago, a group of children ages 7 to 12 were asked to name as many presidents and brands of alcoholic beverages as they could. On average, they named 4.8 presidents and 5.2 beverages (Edward Klein, "The Best and Worst of Everything," *Parade*, 30 December 1990, 5).

I Thinking criticaLLy about the
nternet

"LET THE BROWSER BEWARE!"

"SURF AT YOUR OWN RISK"

Don't expect to find these warnings on the Internet. The ideas you find there have not been screened by a board of standards for accuracy or reasonableness. No logic police force patrols the Internet looking for violators. It is up to you to avoid being victimized. The critical thinking strategy you have been using throughout this book is your best protection. Here are the most important questions to ask whenever you use the Internet.

Whose site is this?

You will likely visit many different sites, including government (.gov), education (.edu), and commercial (.com) sites. Each site will reflect the bias and/or agenda of the people who created and maintain it. Knowing whose site it is will help you evaluate the reliability of the information you find there.

What function does the site serve?

Every site has a specific purpose. Generally speaking, government and education sites are designed to provide the public with important or helpful information. In contrast, commercial sites are designed to sell products and/or services.

Expect the companies that have commercial web sites to say good things about their own products and services and to ignore shortcomings and flaws. Don't be surprised if they imply that their competitors' products and services are inferior. Be aware that such statements and implications may or may not be true and should be tested rather than taken at face value.

Which statements are fact and which are opinion?

A fact is a generally accepted reality, a matter that informed people agree about. An opinion, on the other hand, is a belief or a conclusion open to dispute. Once we accept something as a fact, we are no longer inclined to think critically about it. That is why it is important not to confuse opinion with fact.

Such confusion is potentially greater on the Internet than in print or broadcast media because the dissemination of ideas is easier on the Internet. Anyone can say anything on the Internet and reach a worldwide audience. Not surprisingly, rumor-mongers, manipulators, and other mischief makers have flocked there.

To keep your critical thinking sharp, regard all statements as opinions unless you are certain they are universally endorsed.

Where can statements of fact be confirmed?

Statements that are offered as factual may in reality be false. (Even honest people make mistakes, and not everyone is honest.) Suppose you encounter the statement "The divorce rate has tripled in the past 20 years." This is clearly a *statement* of fact. But is it factual? In other words, is it accurate? Prudence suggests that you seek confirmation by looking in an almanac or other statistical record.

The nature of the statement will determine where you can find verification. To confirm the statement that a congressional candidate was once convicted of sexual harassment, for example, you would check appropriate court records or, at the very least, determine what other sources, if any, support the claim. Endorsement of the statement by the candidate's opponents would mean little; admission by his or her political *allies* would be significant.

How widely shared is this opinion? What do authorities on the subject think of it?

Knowing whether an opinion is shared by a majority or a minority will not tell you how reasonable it is. Minority opinions are not necessarily inferior. Many great insights can be traced to a single individual's advancing an unpopular view. But for every minority view that eventually is proven right, several are proven wrong.

To put it simply, the odds favor the consensus views of informed people. Identify the full range of opinions on the issue by consulting other Internet web sites that deal with the topic in question. (Also, consult print and broadcast media sources.) Hesitate to accept any opinion that is rejected by most informed people, as well as any opinion about which informed people are sharply divided.

Is the reasoning behind the opinion logical?

Look specifically for the following errors, which were discussed in Chapter Five, "Recognizing Errors in Thinking." Each of them can be found in many places, including web sites:

Errors of perception: "mine is better" thinking, selective perception, gullibility and skepticism, bias toward the majority or the minority, pretending to know, bias for or against change, either/or thinking

Errors of judgment: double standard, irrelevant criterion, overgeneralizing or stereotyping, hasty conclusion, unwarranted assumption, failure to make a distinction, oversimplification

Errors of reaction: explaining away, shifting the burden of proof, attacking the person, straw man

Does the evidence support the opinion?

In making this decision, consider all the evidence you have found. That includes the evidence offered in support of the opinion and the evidence you found in searching the Internet and other information sources. Remember, too, that your own personal observation and experience, if relevant to the issue, count as evidence.

Exercise 72

Visit each of the following web sites. Browse through the various "departments," to determine what kinds of investigation the site would be most helpful with. (Don't rush—the prominent parts of a site are not always the most useful.) Then write a summary of your findings.

a) www.askjeeves.com

_____

_____

_____

_____

_____

b) www.about.com

_____

_____

_____

_____

_____

c) www.yahoo.com

_____

_____

_____

_____

_____

d) www.webmd.com

_____

_____

_____

_____

_____

e) www.quicken.com

_____

_____

_____

_____

_____

f) www.mapquest.com

_____

_____

_____

_____

_____

g) www.anywho.com

_____

_____

_____

_____

_____

h) www.google.com

_____

_____

_____

_____

_____

i) www.planetfeedback.com

_____
_____
_____
_____
_____

j) www.weather.com

_____
_____
_____
_____
_____

k) www.infoplease.com

_____
_____
_____
_____
_____

Exercise 73

We tend to take airline safety for granted. But when a serious accident occurs, especially one that claims lives, the public begins questioning how safe air travel is. The issue has many facets, including the age and condition of aircraft, the quality of maintenance, and the adequacy of safety equipment such as radar. Investigate this issue on the Internet, being careful to consider both pro and con arguments. Next, on a separate sheet of paper, report the sites you consulted and what you found there. Finally, apply the critical thinking strategy explained in this chapter, evaluating your findings and stating both your conclusion and the reasoning that led you to it.

Exercise 74

The issue of term limits concerns whether elected officials at the local, state, and/or national levels should be allowed to remain in office indefinitely or be limited to, say, two or three consecutive terms. Investigate this issue on the Internet, being careful to consider both pro and con arguments. Next, on a separate sheet of paper, report the sites you consulted and what you found there. Finally, apply the critical thinking strategy explained in this chapter, evaluating your findings and stating both your conclusion and the reasoning that led you to it.

Exercise 75

Although sex education has been a part of most elementary and secondary curriculums for many years, it remains controversial. There has been sharp division on a number of matters including these:
a) Is sex education helping to solve the problem of teen pregnancy or aggravating it?
b) Do the methods and materials used in sex education support or challenge community standards?
c) Should parents be given a larger role in the development of sex education programs?
Investigate these and related questions on the Internet, being careful to consider both pro and con arguments. Next, on a separate sheet of paper, report the sites you consulted and what you found there. Finally, apply the critical thinking strategy explained in this chapter, evaluating your findings and stating both your conclusion and the reasoning that led you to it. See **http://www.hmco.com/college** for links to this exercise.

Exercise 76

Suppose you've decided to buy a new car and need to find the best terms on an auto loan. Search the Internet, identify a number of lenders, and compare the terms they offer. Summarize your findings on a separate sheet of paper. Then decide which lender would be the best one for you and explain your reasoning.

Practicing Critical Thinking 18

On a separate sheet of paper, select an observation you have made since beginning this chapter and reflect on it as you have previous observations. (If you prefer, select an observation you recorded in a previous chapter but never analyzed.)

Name _____ Date _____ /_____ /_____

1 Newton Minow believes that television has improved significantly over the past quarter-century. True or False? Explain.

2 Identify some common criticisms of magazine publishing.

3 The first newspaper was published in the nineteenth century. True or False? Explain.

4 Identify some criticisms commonly made of popular music.

5 Define each of the following terms:

Bandwagon

Glittering generality

Empty comparison

Meaningless slogan

Testimonial

Transfer

Stacking the deck

Misleading statement

6 Identify some criticisms commonly made of print advertising.

7 The function of most commercial web sites is to provide a public service. True or False? Explain.

8 Name the three biases that can corrupt your thinking about research.

9 Name five elements to examine when evaluating a movie.

Answers to this quiz may be found at http://college.hmco.com.

7

Expressing Ideas Persuasively

What is persuasion?

You and a friend are discussing a controversial issue. She states her view and the reasoning behind it. You disagree and explain your position. When you are finished, she says with great enthusiasm, "You're so right. I see the issue clearly now. I don't know how I could have reached such a silly conclusion. Thanks for helping me see my error."

Have you ever had such an experience? Probably not. People don't abandon their opinions that easily. Whether their minds work quickly or slowly, meticulously or carelessly, once they get an idea, they are reluctant to let go of it.

Persuasion is the art of lowering people's natural resistance to ideas that challenge their own.

Many of the exercises you completed in previous chapters involved persuasion. In other words, they challenged you to gain other people's acceptance of your ideas.

For example, in Exercise 1 you stated and explained whether Galileo's finding that the earth revolved around the sun was true only for him or was objectively true—that is, true always and for everyone.

In Exercise 9 you evaluated a series of brief arguments such as "Women should not take their husbands' names when they marry. Doing so is a sign of subjugation." And in Exercise 22 you decided whether a statement like "The offender never forgives" was completely true, partly true, or completely false.

The art of persuasion consists of a number of strategies, which we will discuss in this chapter. But you should understand at the outset that these strategies carry no guarantee of success. No matter how brilliantly you apply them, the person you are trying to persuade will always remain free to reject your view.

If the strategies of persuasion do not guarantee success, why are they considered important? Because they greatly *increase the odds* of your getting a fair hearing for your ideas.

When does persuasion occur? For some strange reason, we often expect an immediate sign that our persuasive efforts have been successful. Invariably that expectation leads to disappointment. People don't routinely change their minds. And when they do, it is usually only after considerable reflection. Your attempt to persuade today may not bear fruit for days, weeks, or months.

In some cases so much time will have passed that the person will forget that the idea she now holds was initially presented by you. She may think of it as her own original idea! Don't take such a reaction personally. Instead, be encouraged that your persuasive effort proved successful.

Guidelines for persuasion

Previous chapters presented guidelines for critical thinking. Here you will learn some helpful guidelines for expressing your thinking persuasively. The focus will be on persuasive *writing*. However, the same guidelines apply to persuasive *speaking*. For additional information on persuasion, ask your campus librarian to recommend a good composition handbook.

The basic principle of persuasion is the Golden Rule: "Do unto others as you would have them do unto you." Among the most important applications of this rule are the following:

If you expect your views to be understood, make the effort to understand other people's views.

If you expect others to support their views with evidence, support yours with evidence.

If you expect other people to answer your questions, answer theirs.

If you don't like being ridiculed, don't ridicule others.

If you are upset when others misquote you, take care not to misquote them.

The guidelines of persuasion are as follows:

Guideline 1: Complete the thinking process

Some people begin their persuasive writing hoping to develop their thoughts about the issue as they are writing. The result is usually a confused, disorganized, unpersuasive composition.

You can avoid this fate. Before presenting your ideas to others, analyze the issue using the critical thinking approach you learned in earlier chapters. Know what you think about the issue and the evidence for your view. (During the thinking stage, of course you may use writing as a tool of discovery and analysis—for example, for recording thoughts and impressions.)

The conclusion you reach about the issue will be the controlling idea of your composition.

The example of Jennifer in Chapter One illustrates how a controlling idea is developed. Remember, Jennifer directed her critical thinking to the subject of astrology. After doing so she concluded that even though many well-known, educated people believe in astrology, it is a poor guide to everyday living.

If Jennifer were writing a persuasive composition, that conclusion would be her controlling idea. Everything else in her composition would serve to support that idea and present it effectively.

Guideline 2: Understand your audience

The audience for persuasive writing is typically mixed. Some readers will agree thoroughly with your view; others will partly agree and partly disagree; still others will disagree entirely. Writing for those who agree is no challenge. Writing for those who partly agree is difficult because you have no sure way of knowing where their agreement ends and their disagreement begins. For this reason, it is best to write for those who disagree entirely. They will always be your most critical readers.

Disagreement, of course, may take a variety of forms, and each may be based on a different rationale. Thus your most prudent approach is to become familiar with *all views of the issue that oppose your view.* Then you should ask:

1. What questions and challenges would people who hold those competing views raise about my view?

2. What are the most reasonable answers to those questions?

The better your answers and the more solid your evidence, the greater your chance of persuading those who disagree with you. Keep in mind that any change that takes place in their thinking will not be instantaneous and that if and when such a change occurs, you will not have made it for them. You will merely have provided a reason for them to make it themselves.

Guideline 3: Support your judgments with evidence

In persuasive writing, what you think is important. Yet the evidence that supports what you think is even more important. Getting others to change their views will take more than your say-so. Careful thinkers want good reasons for changing their minds.

You may recall that Jennifer supported her judgment on astrology with these reasons:

1. It is based on such superstitious beliefs as the association of the red planet, Mars, with blood and aggression.

2. It considers birth, rather than conception, as the time of greatest planetary influence. (This view ignores the basic principles of biology.)

3. Its central tenet of planetary influence has not been modified as new planets have been discovered.

If Jennifer were writing a persuasive paper, she would present these reasons in more detail. She might also anticipate questions such as these: Is astrology based on other superstitions? What exactly do astrologers say about planetary influence at birth? Do they ever mention genetics? Why did the discovery of new planets require that the planetary influence idea be modified?

Jennifer could answer these questions and consider other approaches. For example, she could discuss research studies, introduce examples of specific horoscope advice from history, and quote or paraphrase authorities on the subject of astrology.

You may find one or more of these approaches useful in your persuasive writing (and speaking).

Guideline 4: Choose a suitable organization

A simple, effective way to organize a persuasive composition is to present your information in the following order:

1. Your controlling idea

2. Your first argument for this idea, with supporting evidence

3. Your second argument and supporting evidence

4. Your third argument (if you have one) and supporting evidence

Writers often put their most powerful argument last to make readers' final impression especially positive.

If you choose to use a formal introduction, place it before the controlling idea. Likewise, if you want to have a formal conclusion to sum up or reinforce your message, place it after your last argument.

Guideline 5: Express your ideas effectively

Style is less important than substance. Even so, style can build or destroy readers' confidence in you. These style rules will help you make your writing clear and appealing:

1. **Choose words that convey your idea exactly.** Avoid using long or fancy words just to impress your readers.

2. **Cut unnecessary words.** When you can, reduce a sentence to a clause, a clause to a phrase, a phrase to a word.

3. **Vary your sentences.** Occasionally combine several short sentences into a longer one. Begin sentences in different ways by changing the order of phrases and clauses. For example, you could change "He studied hard because he wanted to graduate with honors" to "Because he wanted to graduate with honors, he studied hard."

4. **Vary your paragraph length.** Having paragraphs that are all the same length is monotonous. Make the length between five and fifteen lines, aiming for an average of ten lines. To keep the flow of your ideas clear, break paragraphs between ideas rather than in the middle of an idea.

Guideline 6: Proofread for punctuation, grammar, and usage

Professional writers make as many errors as amateurs. The difference is that professionals proofread and correct their work before others see it. Their example is worth imitating.

Any English instructor will be able to recommend a guide to punctuation, grammar, and usage. If it is not in stock in your campus bookstore, the staff will be able to order it for you.

Most word processors offer spellchecking, and some can also check for grammar and usage. But not all programs are equally comprehensive or reliable. Rather than depend entirely on your word processor for proofreading, you should develop this skill yourself.

Being persuasive in school

Like most students, you probably consider examinations the educational equivalent of a medical checkup. Your instructors examine the contents of your mind and make a diagnosis: "Your geography 'count' is excellent" or "You are seriously deficient in sociology." You may even receive some unpleasant medicine—"I'm prescribing that you repeat the course."

Notice that in this scenario your role is passive. You submit to the ordeal and then await the outcome. Your instructors have all the power.

But there is a different way to consider examinations—as opportunities for persuasion. From this perspective, your role is active rather than passive. You have the power to shape the conclusions your teachers reach about you. In this sense, you are the teacher and they are the learners.

This new way of regarding examinations is especially relevant to essay examinations, in which you are required to do more than merely circle the right answer.

Suppose you encountered the following question on an essay exam:

Jones and Smith have advanced different theories of learning. Compare and evaluate these theories.

Your first task is to demonstrate that you are familiar with the theories and the similarities and differences between them. Your second task is to decide whether one theory is preferable to the other and to persuade the teacher that your decision is reasonable.

Now consider another essay question of a type commonly found on examinations:

Identify three factors that played a role in the outbreak of the Civil War. Which, in your judgment, is the most significant?

What can you do to make your essay persuasive? First, choose factors that historians consider truly important. Second, provide evidence that demonstrates the importance of each. Third, make a strong and reasonable case that the one factor you *say* is most significant really *is* so.

Examinations are not your only chance to be persuasive. Every class discussion offers an additional opportunity.

Let's say your sociology class is discussing the possible relationship between divorce and juvenile delinquency. You and your classmates will probably have done the same background reading. You will all be able to state, more or less clearly, what the various authors said and the evidence they provided to support their ideas.

Where will you and your classmates *differ?* You will differ in what each of you thinks about the subject and about the various views expressed by the authors. Your challenge will be to present your ideas so compellingly that classmates who began by disagreeing with you end by agreeing.

The guidelines for persuasion will help you meet the challenges of both examinations and classroom discussions.

Being persuasive in the workplace

The challenge to be persuasive in the workplace arises even before you have a job. It begins during the job interview. The unspoken question in every interviewer's mind is "Why should I hire this person?"

As important as the résumé is in presenting your credentials, the way you conduct yourself during the interview is even more critical. Your answers to the questions asked of you, the questions you raise, and the information you present about your training, work experience, and dedication will strongly influence the interviewer's decision.

Once you are on the job, opportunities to be persuasive occur daily—in some cases hourly. Here are just a few examples that are occurring at this very moment·

- A car salesperson is attempting to finalize a deal with a customer.
- A stockbroker is explaining to a client why a change in investment strategy is advisable.
- A customer service representative is attempting to persuade an irate customer to continue doing business with the company despite an unpleasant experience.
- A representative of one of the long-distance companies is on the phone urging someone to switch to his company.
- An inventor is trying to sell her latest invention to a company.

- A corporate official is addressing stockholders at an annual meeting in the hope of convincing them that the profit statistics are more encouraging than they appear.

- A junior executive is presenting her idea for a new product line to her superiors.

- A supervisor is appealing to his staff for more cooperation and teamwork in the office.

- An executive is sitting in a bank official's office attempting to secure a business loan.

And at this very moment, thousands of people are sitting face to face with their bosses trying to make the case for a promotion or a pay raise.

All these individuals are more likely to be successful in their attempts at persuading others if they understand the guidelines for persuasion and apply them conscientiously. You are too.

Keep in mind that the challenge of persuading others is greater in spoken than in written communication. Printed words can be studied again and again; the spoken word, once uttered, is gone. Also, speaking is less formal and precise and therefore more easily misunderstood.

Be sure to pay special attention to the guidelines in speaking situations. Think through the problem or issue in advance of the meeting. Review your evidence so you can present it clearly and effectively. Try to anticipate and evaluate the arguments others could present.

These preparations are in no way a substitute for listening to others and giving their ideas a fair hearing. If you have developed your viewpoint carefully, it is understandable that you will feel strongly about it. Still, if you want others to be open to your efforts at persuasion, you should be willing to be equally open to theirs.

Being persuasive in the community

Persuasion is not just for school and work. It also applies in your various roles in your neighborhood, town, or city. You undoubtedly have a number of such roles. You may be a Little League coach, a den mother, a hospital volunteer, a "Big Brother" or "Big Sister," or a member of a service organization or church council.

In any of these roles you are bound to encounter issues—that is, subjects about which the people around you have different opinions. Even issues of seemingly slight significance can stir people's passions and generate spirited debate. Should Little Leaguers be required to buy full uniforms? Would Friday evening or Saturday afternoon be the best time for the sale? The guidelines for persuasion will be helpful in such situations.

Your community, in the larger sense, goes beyond neighborhood and municipality. You are also a citizen of a state, a nation, and the world. What happens anywhere on the planet could have an impact on your life. You therefore have good reason to be interested in, and form opinions about, the social, economic, and political issues of the day.

One issue that has received considerable attention in recent years concerns Microsoft Corporation and the Internet. The U.S. Justice Department filed an antitrust action against Microsoft. One of the charges was that the company was using "predatory" business practices. By bundling its Internet Explorer with Windows 98, the government said, Microsoft gained an unfair advantage over its competitors. The result, in the government's view, would be a monopoly for Microsoft and potential harm to the public interest. The government demanded that Microsoft either remove its Internet Explorer from Windows 98 or add its competitor Netscape Communications' browser.

Microsoft Chairman Bill Gates said that the demand was like "requiring Coca-Cola to include three cans of Pepsi in every six-pack." By itself that striking analogy probably led many people to conclude that Gates was right and the government was wrong.

But the government's chief antitrust agent, Joel Klein, had an interesting analogy of his own. He said it is as if Coke had control of all the shelves in the grocery store and didn't allow Pepsi to be sold there.

The more you read about this issue, the more you will realize that there are good arguments on both sides. So it is with most controversies. That is why the guidelines of persuasion are so important.

Step 1:   "Complete the thinking process" ensures that you understand all sides of the issue.

Step 2:   "Understand your audience" enables you to anticipate how others are likely to respond to your view.

Step 3:   "Support your judgments with evidence" guides you to demonstrate the soundness of your view.

Steps 4 through 6:   In regard to organization, expression, and correctness, ensure that your presentation is easy to follow and free of distracting elements. Remember that people who already disagree with you are ready to dismiss your argument for the smallest reason.

Being persuasive in relationships

A close friend has decided to drop out of school after receiving a disappointing grade in a course in her major field. You know she is a talented person and believe that dropping out of school would be a serious mistake. What do you do?

Many people, perhaps a majority, would rattle off every reason they could think of for her to stay in school, hoping against hope that one of those reasons would convince her to do so. "People will call you a quitter if you drop out." "Your enemies will be overjoyed." "Your friends will be saddened." "Your parents will be disappointed." "You won't be able to find a decent job." And so on.

The guidelines for persuasion offer a more thoughtful approach, one with greater potential for success. Here's how you might use them in this case.

Your first step would be to listen—*really* listen—to her story and then ask questions such as these:

1. *Did you receive a failing grade or merely one that is lower than you are accustomed to receiving?* Outstanding students sometimes consider a low passing grade such as a D or a C to be failing, when in fact it is not. They may also reason that a single low grade ruins one's chances for academic success, which is not the case.

2. *Did you ask your professor to review your grade?* A request for a review of the grade is not unreasonable. Like the rest of us, professors sometimes make mistakes.

3. *Did you talk to the professor about your low grade?* She may find that despite the low grade, the professor takes a generally favorable view of her potential in the field.

4. *Have you considered any alternatives to quitting school?* One rather obvious alternative is to take the course over again, perhaps engaging a tutor to ensure a better performance.

This thoughtful approach would help you decide the most reasonable course of action for her. Then you would anticipate her likely reaction to the idea and decide what evidence would persuade her. Finally you would rehearse your presentation in your mind. (If your presentation were in a letter or an email rather than in person, you would check the organization, expression, and correctness of your writing.)

The guidelines to persuasion offer a helpful approach to a wide variety of situations that arise in personal relationships. Here are just a few examples:

Healing a breach between two friends by persuading one or both to forgive and forget

Getting a loved one to drive more carefully

Teaching children to be more considerate of one another

Encouraging a loved one to quit smoking or to drink more responsibly

Exercise 77

Describe a school situation—for example, in the classroom or a campus organization—in which you were challenged to be persuasive. Revisit that situation, apply the guidelines for persuasion, and explain how you would deal with it if it were occurring now. (Feel free to substitute a present situation for a past one if you wish.)

_____

_____

_____

_____

_____

_____

_____

_____

_____

_____

_____

_____

Exercise 78

Describe a work situation in which you were challenged to be persuasive. Revisit that situation, apply the guidelines for persuasion, and explain how you would deal with it if it were occurring now. (Feel free to
substitute a present situation for a past one if you wish.)

_____

_____

_____

_____

_____

_____

_____

_____

_____

_____

_____

Exercise 79

In the section "Being persuasive in the Community" the U.S. Department of Justice's case against Microsoft was mentioned. Investigate that case using all the resources at your disposal, including the Internet. Then decide what view of this issue is the most reasonable and, on a separate sheet of paper, write a persuasive composition presenting that view. Be sure to list the sources you consulted.

Exercise 80

Affirmative action was originally intended to solve the problem of discrimination in schools, government, and business. However, many people believe it has created "reverse" discrimination. This new view resulted in both the state of California's banning affirmative action in its university system and the successful ballot initiative known as Proposition 209, which ended affirmative action in all state and local government programs in California.

Champions of affirmative action maintain that it redresses past grievances, helps today's minorities overcome victimization, and benefits society by promoting fairness in the workplace. Opponents claim that it devalues merit, diminishes genuine achievement, and does a disservice to minority and majority alike.

It is important to note that the division of viewpoints does not always follow racial or ethnic lines. For example, the leader of the campaign against affirmative action in the University of California system was Ward Connerly, an African American.

Investigate that case using all the resources at your disposal, including the Internet. Then decide what view of this issue is the most reasonable and, on a separate sheet of paper, write a persuasive composition presenting that view. Be sure to list the sources you consulted.

Exercise 81

Contemporary feminism is divided into two main camps—"gender" feminism and "equity" feminism. Gender feminists include Gloria Steinem
and Patricia Ireland. Equity feminists include Christina Hoff Sommers
and Camille Paglia. The two camps take very different views of the
many issues of special interest to women, including the question of
what the women's movement's agenda should be.

Investigate the differences between the two camps using all the resources at your disposal, including the Internet. Then decide which side
you are most in agreement with and, on a separate sheet of paper, write
a persuasive composition presenting your view. Be sure to list the
sources you consulted.

Exercise 82

Describe a personal relationship in which you have faced a challenge to
be persuasive—for example, a situation involving a friend or a family
member. Then apply the guidelines for persuasion and write a letter or
an email to that person.

Name _____ Date _____ /_____ /_____

1   What is persuasion?

2   The strategies of persuasion guarantee that you will be successful. True or
    False? Explain.

3   If persuasion occurs at all, it occurs immediately after you present your ideas.
    True or False? Explain.

4   The challenge of persuading others is greater in spoken communication than in
    written communication. True or False? Explain.

5 Identify the six guidelines for persuasion:

1.

2.

3.

4.

5.

6.

6 Identify the four areas in which the guidelines for persuasion may be used.

Answers to this quiz may be found at http://college.hmco.com.

EpiLogue

make the end a beginning

You've finished reading this book and completed its exercises and other opportunities to practice critical thinking. Now you have a choice. You can decide that this moment will mark the end of one more academic experience. If this is your choice, just consign the book to a box in your basement and let it gather dust. As memory fades, the experiences you had with this book will be lost.

There is an alternative. You can decide to make this book and critical thinking skills a vital part of your life. You can choose to make the end a beginning. One strategy is to buy a notebook and continue the journal you began here. As explained in Chapter One, a bound notebook no smaller than 6 × 9 inches is preferable. Use the left pages for recording observations; reserve the right pages for reflections on those observations. Since reflections are usually lengthier than observations, leave appropriate space between observations.

Here is a collection of quotations to help you get started. Some apply in many situations, others in a limited number. A few may need qualification. All will provide excellent food for thought. *Bon appétit!*

If I am not for myself, who will be? If I am only for myself, what am I?
—Rabbi Hillel

Someone's boring me . . . I think it's me. —Dylan Thomas

A great many people think they are thinking when they are merely rearranging their prejudices. —William James

Each morning puts a man on trial and each evening passes judgment.
—Roy L. Smith

There are two ways of exerting one's strength: one is pushing down, and the other is pulling up. —Booker T. Washington

Happiness is not a state to arrive at, but a manner of traveling.
—Margaret Lee Rumbeck

How glorious it is—and how painful—to be an exception. —Alfred de Musset

The man who most vividly realizes a difficulty is the man most likely to overcome it. —Joseph Farrell

You can tell the ideals of a nation by its advertisements. —Norman Douglas

To escape criticism—do nothing, say nothing, be nothing.   —Elbert G. Hubbard

That man is the richest whose pleasures are the cheapest.
   —Henry David Thoreau

To read without reflecting is like eating without digesting.   —Edmund Burke

Remember, no one can make you feel inferior without your consent.
   —Eleanor Roosevelt

Bibliography

The following books on critical thinking and related subjects can help you deepen your understanding and expand your skill.

Adams, James. *Conceptual Blockbusting.* W. W. Norton, New York, 1979.

Adler, Mortimer.

How to Read a Book. Simon and Schuster, New York, 1972.

Intellect: Mind Over Matter. Macmillan Publishing Co., New York, 1990.

Barker, Evelyn M. *Everyday Reasoning.* Prentice-Hall, Englewood Cliffs, NJ, 1981.

Barry, Vincent E., and Joel Rudinow. *Invitation to Critical Thinking.* Holt, Rinehart & Winston, New York, 1990.

Browne, Neil, and Stuart Keely. *Asking the Right Questions: A Guide to Critical Thinking.* Prentice-Hall, Englewood Cliffs, NJ, 1993.

Cederblom, J. B., and Paulsen, David W. *Critical Reasoning.* Wadsworth Publishing Co., Belmont, CA, 1996.

Chaffee, John. *Thinking Critically.* Houghton-Mifflin, New York, 1997.

Damer, Edward. *Attacking Faulty Reasoning.* Wadsworth Publishing Co., Belmont, CA, 1987.

DeBono, Edward. *Lateral Thinking.* Harper & Row, New York, 1970.

Engel, S. Morris. *With Good Reason: An Introduction to Informal Fallacies.* Third Edition. St. Martin's Press, New York, 1994.

Fisher, Alec. *The Logic of Real Arguments.* Cambridge University Press, New York, 1988.

Govier, Trudy. *A Practical Study of Argument.* Wadsworth Publishing Co., Belmont, CA, 1992.

Halpern, Diane. *Thought and Knowledge.* Lawrence Erlbaum, Hillsdale, NJ, 1989.

Hitchcock, David. *Critical Thinking: A Guide to Evaluating Information.* Methuen Publications, Toronto, Canada, 1983.

Hoaglund, John. *Critical Thinking.* Vale Press, Newport News, VA, 1995.

Johnson, Ralph, and J. A. Blair. *Logical Self-Defense.* McGraw-Hill, New York, 1994.

Kytle, Ray. *Clear Thinking for Composition.* McGraw-Hill Book Co., New York, 1987.

Lazere, Donald. *American Media and Mass Culture.* University of California Press, Berkeley, CA, 1987.

Mander, Jerry. *Four Arguments for the Elimination of Television.* Quill Publishing, New York, 1978.

Mayfield, Marlys. *Thinking for Yourself: Developing Critical Thinking Skills Through Reading and Writing.* Wadsworth Publishing Co., Belmont, CA, 1997.

Michalos, Alex C. *Improving Your Reasoning.* Prentice-Hall, Englewood Cliffs, New Jersey, 1986.

Miller, Robert K. *Informed Argument.* Harcourt Brace Jovanovich, San Diego, CA, 1997.

Missimer, Connie. *Good Arguments.* Prentice-Hall, Englewood Cliffs, NJ, 1994.

Moore, Brooke N. *Critical Thinking: Evaluating Claims and Arguments in Everyday Life.* Mayfield Publishing Co., Palo Alto, CA, 1986.

Moore, Edgar. *Creative and Critical Reasoning.* Houghton Mifflin Co., Boston, MA, 1984.

Nickerson, Raymond S. *Reflections on Reasoning.* Lawrence Erlbaum, Hillsdale, NJ, 1986.

Nosich, Gerald. *Reasons and Arguments.* Wadsworth Publishing Co., Belmont, CA, 1982.

Paul, Richard. *Critical Thinking: What Every Person Needs to Survive in a Rapidly Changing World.* Center for Critical Thinking and Moral Critique, Sonoma State University, Rohnert Park, CA, 1995.

Perkins, David. *Knowledge as Design.* Lawrence Erlbaum, Hillsdale, NJ, 1986.

Postman, Neil. *Amusing Ourselves to Death.* Oxford University Press, New York, 1985.

Rosenthal, Peggy. *Words and Values.* Oxford University Press, New York, 1984.

Ruggiero, Vincent Ryan.

> *Thinking Critically About Ethical Issues.* Mayfield Publishing Co., Mountain View, CA, 1992.

> *Warning: Nonsense Is Destroying America.* Thomas Nelson, Nashville, TN, 1994.

> *Beyond Feelings: A Guide to Critical Thinking.* Mayfield Publishing Co., Mountain View, CA, 1995.

> *The Art of Thinking.* Fourth Edition. HarperCollins, New York, 1995.

Scriven, Michael. *Reasoning.* McGraw-Hill, New York, 1997.

Seech, Zachary. *Open Minds and Everyday Reasoning.* Wadsworth Publishing Co., Belmont, CA, 1993.

Shor, Ira. *Critical Thinking and Everyday Life.* University of Chicago Press, Chicago, IL, 1987.

Siegel, Harvey. *Relativism Refuted.* Kluwer-Academic Publishers, Norwell, MA, 1987.

Toulmin, Stephen. *The Uses of Argument*. Cambridge University Press, New York, 1958.

Toulmin, Stephen E., Richard Rieke, and Alan Janik. *An Introduction to Reasoning*. Macmillan Publishing Co., New York, 1979.

Von Oech, Roger.

   A Kick in the Seat of the Pants. Harper & Row, New York, 1986.

   A Whack on the Side of the Head. HarperCollins, New York, 1993.

Weddle, Perry. *Argument*. McGraw-Hill, New York, 1978.

Index

About the Author (library item to come from customer)

Vincent Ryan Ruggiero is an internationally known writer, lecturer, and consultant whose areas of special interest and expertise are critical and creative thinking, ethics, educational reform, and social criticism.

A pioneer in the movement to make thinking skills instruction an important emphasis at every level of education, he holds the rank of Professor Emeritus, State University of New York at Delhi, and resides in Dunedin, Florida.

Professor Ruggiero's nineteen books include *Beyond Feelings: A Guide to Critical Thinking, Thinking Critically About Ethical Issues, The Art of Thinking, Teaching Thinking Across the Curriculum, A Guide to Thinking Sociologically,* and *Warning: Nonsense Is Destroying America.*